SANSKRIT PROSODY

AND

NUMERICAL SYMBOLS EXPLAINED

SANSKRIT PROSODY

AND

NUMERICAL SYMBOLS EXPLAINED

CHARLES PHILIP BROWN

GYAN

Published by

Gyan Publishing House
5, Ansari Road
Daryaganj, New Delhi-110002
Phone: 011-47034999, 9811692060
E-mail: books@gyanbooks.com

Distribution Network
gyanbooks.com
India, USA, Canada, UK, Australia

ISBN: 978-93-7014-236-7 (PB)

First Published, 1869

2nd Impression 2025

Printed at: Gyan Press, Delhi.

SANSKRIT PROSODY AND NUMERICAL SYMBOLS EXPLAINED
Author: CHARLES PHILIP BROWN

SANSKRIT PROSODY EXPLAINED.

SANSKRIT PROSODY

AND

NUMERICAL SYMBOLS

EXPLAINED

BY CHARLES PHILIP BROWN, M.R.A.S.

AUTHOR OF A TELUGU DICTIONARY, GRAMMAR, ETC. PROFESSOR OF TELUGU IN THE UNIVERSITY OF LONDON.

NOBIS PRIMA SIT VIRTUS PERSPICUITAS.

—*Quinctil.* viii. 2.

LONDON:

TRÜBNER & Co., 60, PATERNOSTER ROW.

MDCCCLXIX.

PREFACE.

SANSKRIT LITERATURE is chiefly in verse. The poems and plays, the histories and legends, treatises on law, divinity, astronomy, mathematicks, and indeed nearly all literature being in metre. The "Prosody is easy and beautiful," says Sir William Jones. "It is infinitely more rich and more varied," observes the learned Chézy, "than that of Greek; and has no syllables of doubtful quantity." The venerable Colebrooke (Essays ii. 62) speaks of the aid it affords in deciphering passages rendered obscure by the inaccuracy of the transcripts: he notices that the artifice of its construction is peculiar, and not devoid of ingenuity; and it is richer than that of any other language. Yet many who have attempted the study in India, guided by a Pandit, complain that the art is intricate. Indeed most of the aspirants have been disheartened (as I was at first); for the Prosody is overlaid with a profusion of pedantic refinements, arithmetical and superstitious. Most of the rules in the Sanskrit Prosodies are intended to guide composers, not learners.

In 1827, at Madras, at the desire of the College Board, I printed a short account of Telugu and Sanskrit Prosody. Ten years after, when I was in London, the learned Professor Rosen, who had edited Colebrooke's Essays, requested me to prepare a statement which he printed in the Asiatic Journal for 1837. This fell into the hands of a young German at Konigsberg who had been reading Sanskrit for two years: and encouraged him. In 1855 Professor Wilson introduced him to me in London: he was Professor Theodor Goldstücker, whose skill in Sanskrit lore has in late years been acknowledged by learned brahmans in Bengal, Benares, and Lahore. He called upon me to prepare an easier and more complete volume for the use of students. Accordingly I have written the rules again, addressing the explanations to the beginner: who now can learn more in ten days than a pandit could have taught him in ten years.

Professor Francis Johnson has with his usual kindness superintended the printing of these pages.

Numerical Symbols are much used in Sanskrit books on Prosody, as well as regarding chronology. Of these I have subjoined an explanation: with some suggestions for a Memoria Technica in English.

C. P. B.

22, Kildare Gardens, London,
April, 1869.

INDEX.

CONTENTS.

ERRATA.

P. 12, line 23, *read* प्रख्या

24, „ 20, „ The Mallet to Destroy Delusion.

SANSKRIT PROSODY EXPLAINED.

INTRODUCTORY REMARKS.

The vowels a, i, u, ri, lu, are short: as in अतिशय atiśaya मिलित milita, युधि yudhi, कृप kṛipa. The rest are long.

Short or breve is called लघु lag-hu or ह्रस्व hraswa, meaning 'light.' Long is called गुरु guru 'heavy,' or दीर्घ dīrgha 'long.'

A breve becomes guru if followed by two consonants, as 'a' in अस्ति asti, or वक्र vakra. But the vowels Ṛi and Ḷri do not lengthen the preceding vowel. Thus सकृत् săkṛit.

A breve is marked with an upright line '।' thus; a tribrach, which we write ∪∪∪ is marked ।।।. The long mark is ∪ which we use for a breve. In Dēvanāgari the character resembles the Persian hamza (ء), in Bengali is similar to the number for six in that alphabet.

But the language is pronounced as it is written, and the quantity of each syllable is evident to the eye: the marks for long and breve are therefore seldom used.

The letter य Y is always a consonant, and requires a vowel, as in दैत्यः dait-yah, कार्यं kār-yám, योगिन् yogin, शय्या śayyā. When the consonant म M is final, as in नलम् अब्रवीत् Nalăm + abravīt, it does not suffer elision. (Nala. iv. 1).

Prosody is called छन्दः chhandah, that is, 'fancy, will, pleasure.'

Sanskrit Prosody is measured with feet, called gaṇa, denoted by letters, Ma, Ya, Ra, etc. fixed in days earlier than the Homeric age. M or Ma denoted a foot of three long syllables, as 'majestas' or 'Longini' or 'has sylvas.' Na is a tribrach of three breves like 'mulier' or 'avibus.' Eight such feet are given in the गणप्रस्तारः or Table. To each I have added a Sanskrit and a Latin instance, having the same initial.

TABLE OF FEET.

NAME.		SYLLABLES.	EXAMPLE.	
मगणं	Ma	— — —	मन्त्राणां	Mantrāṇām
यगणं	Ya	∪ — —	यथार्थं	Yathārtham
रगणं	Ra	— ∪ —	रक्षणं	Racshaṇam
सगणं	Sa	∪ ∪ —	सहजं	Sahajam
तगणं	Ta	— — ∪	तन्त्राणि	Tantrāṇi
जगणं	Ja	∪ — ∪	जजाप	Jajāpa
भगणं	Bha	— ∪ ∪	भङ्गुर	Bhanguram
नगणं	Na	∪ ∪ ∪	नयति	Nayati

The Greek names, with Latin instances.

NAME.	SYLLABLES.	EXAMPLE.
Molossus	— — —	Mæcenas
Bacchius	∪ — —	'Ymetto
Creticus	— ∪ —	Reddidi
Anapæstus	∪ ∪ —	Similes
Antibacchius	— — ∪	Tentare
Amphibrachys	∪ — ∪	Juvabit
Dactylus	— ∪ ∪	Bucula
Tribrachys	∪ ∪ ∪	Nivea

In the three columns thus arranged in ancient times, the first has a long and a breve alternately; the second has two of each; the third has four.

The dactyl, in the present pages, will be marked B. The spondee will be marked – – as in Latin.

To aid the memory, a learned German friend has given me the following sentence: मायावी यतात्मा रावणः सहसा तन्त्राणि अजाप भावय नहति "The deceitful, self-controlling Ravaṇa uttered his spells in haste, beginning with 'Preserve us'" [from] death.

A long syllable is called Guru गुरु and a breve is लघु la-ghu: and the initials, L, G, are thus used:

गगं	gagam or गा gā	–	–	spondæus.
ललं	la lam or ला lā	∪	∪	pyrrhichius.
गलं	ga lam	–	∪	trochæus.
लगं	lagam	∪	–	iambus.

A line is called pāda or charaṇa, meaning a foot; four such form a padya or slok. A prosodial measure of two or three syllables is called gaṇa गण because it is counted; we call it a foot.

'Aksharam,' a 'letter,' also is a 'syllable.' संस्कृतं Sams-kru-tam, or गीर्वाणं Gīr-vā-nam (another name of the language) are called tri-literal, or words of three syllables. So is Ak-sha-ram.

All syllables are of a definite length, apparent to the eye; none are doubtful.

The last syllable of each line, in the uniform metres, is long by rule; but in practice is free.

"Pluta," denoting 'extension,' is the name given to a quaver or protracted sound, used in chaunting the Vedas. In prosody it is merely a long syllable.

The native treatises are crowded with numerical expressions which make the art mysterious; but such devices merely impede the progress of the learner.

On the Anushṭup.

The Tale of Nala commences thus: each line being divided into four parts.

आसीद्‌ राजा । नलोनाम । वीरसेन । सुतोबली

उपपन्नो । गुणैर्‌ इष्टै । रूपवान्‌ अ । श्वकोविदः

A´síd rājā | Nalō nāma | Vīra sēna | sutō balī

Upapannō | guṇaír ishṭai | rūpavān aś | va kōvidah

This is called the Anushṭup sloka अनुष्टुभ्‌ which some consider the heroic metre. Each line contains sixteen syllables, and two lines are one slôk, or couplet.

There are four syllables in each quarter. The first and third quarters are free from rule: the second usually is ∪ – – with a free syllable: the third has ∪ – ∪ with a free syllable. Marking the free syllables with *x*, the line stands thus:

xxxx ∪ – – *x* *xxxx* ∪ – ∪ *x*

The learner should read several pages aloud, pausing after each quarter: and he will soon perceive the rhythm. After he has accomplished this, he can proceed as follows:

The second foot has five varieties. One is already seen: the others are exemplified in these passages of the same poem:

– – –	Bk II. v. 6.	न्यवेदयत्‌ । ताम्‌ अस्वस्थां	nya vēdayat | tām aswasthām
– ∪ –	I. 3.	अक्षप्रियः । सत्यवादी	acsha priyah | satya vādī
– ∪ ∪	I. 7.	तस्मै प्रस । न्नो दमनः	tasmai prasan | nō damanah
∪ ∪ ∪	XIV. 18.	ब्रह्मर्षिभ्य । श्चभविता	brahmarshibhya | ścha bhavitā

The five feet admissible in the second seat are Ma Ya Ra

Bha Na: which may be recollected in the words Mayūra bhānuh.

In p. 436 of a volume on Sanskrit Grammar printed in 1847, a couplet is quoted from the Laws of Manu:—

Ásīd idam | tamo bhūtam | aprajnātam | a lakshaṇam
a pratarkyam | a vijneyam | prasuptam i | vasarvatah.

And there is added, from the Rāmāyan,

Mā, Nishāda | pratishthām twam | agamah ṣā | ṣwatîh samāh
Yat krauncha mi | thunād ékam | avadhîh kā | ma mohitam

The explanation of the metre there given is erroneous: as are also those of two more instances, there shewn. The student should divide the lines into fours, and he will perceive the metre with ease.

The remaining remarks on the Anushṭup are not intended for beginners.

The rules already given will suffice for most of the slokas found in the Purāṇas. The following rules are observed in the Poems. The instances were selected by a Pandit from the Amara Kosha.

Each half line having eight syllables; the first and last are free, marked *x*; but the other six are subject to rule. Rule regarding the first half.

*x*MY*x*	*x*¯ ¯ ¯ ⏑ ¯ ¯*x*	Utt | hānam paurushē tan | trē
YY	⏑ ¯ ¯ ⏑ ¯ ¯	hrā | dinī vaj ram astrī | syāt
RY	¯ ⏑ ¯ ⏑ ¯ ¯	Pu | lōmajā, Sachīndrā | n′i′
TY	¯ ¯ ⏑ ⏑ ¯ ¯	Sap | tārchir damunāh śu | crah
JY	⏑ ¯ ⏑ ⏑ ¯ ¯	Sa | twaram chapalam túr | ńam
BY	¯ ⏑ ⏑ ⏑ ¯ ¯	Ni | tyāna varatája | sram
MR	¯ ¯ ¯ ¯ ⏑ ¯	Abh | ram mēghō vārivā | hah

*x*YR*x*	*x*∪ – – – ∪ – *x*	E′ | ca yōctyā pushpavan | tau
RR	– ∪ – – ∪ –	Vah | nēr dwayōr jwāla kil | au
RM	– ∪ – – – –	Siv | ā Bhavāni′ Rudrá | ńi′
MB	– – – – ∪ ∪	As | yōdyānam chaitrara | tham
YB	∪ – – – ∪ ∪	Rō | hitáśvō vāyu sa | khah
RB	– ∪ – – ∪ ∪	Kri | pīṭayōnir jvala | nō
TB	– – ∪ – ∪ ∪	Ka | rinyō bhramuh capi | la
MN	– – – ∪ ∪ ∪	Pan | chaité déva tara | vō
YN	∪ – – ∪ ∪ ∪	Gha | na jīmūta mudi | ra
RN	– ∪ – ∪ ∪ ∪	Vās | tōsh patis sura pa | tih
TN	– – ∪ ∪ ∪ ∪	Ka | rinyō bhramu capi | té

These eighteen varieties are found in the first eight syllables: a few other variations occur, but are not approved as harmonious.

The second half, also containing eight syllables, has five variations: the first and last syllables alone remain free from rule.

*x*MJ*x*	*x* – – – ∪ – ∪ *x*	Ag ādhasyá naghá guń | áh
TJ	– – ∪ ∪ – ∪	San | kshiptaih prati samskri | taih
YJ	∪ – – ∪ – ∪	Sa | hachāryach chakutra | chit
BJ	– ∪ ∪ ∪ – ∪	Sarv | āńńamu chi sūda | nah
JJ	∪ – ∪ ∪ – ∪	A | nuśrutya yathāma | ti

This last instance is from Kālidāsa's Jātica Chandrikā.

The halves are independent: any one of the former eighteen may be followed by any one of the latter five.

On Elision.

Each couplet consists of two lines, which in the manuscripts are united, thus (Gita i. 25):

भीष्मद्रोणप्रमुखतः सर्वेषां च महीक्षितामुवाचपार्थ पश्यैतान्समवेतान्कु-

रूनिति । २५ । अथापक्षत्स्थि ताग्पार्थः पितृनथपितामहाणाचार्थ्याभ्रातु-लान् etc.

Again in xv. 3:

अश्वत्थामेतं सुविरूढमूलमसंगशास्त्रेण etc.

Here we see each half is run into one unbroken line: which European scholars divide, at the cæsura, into a couplet.

Where such elision occurs in the specimens now to be cited, two lines will be given: which are alike. Elsewhere a single line suffices.

THE UNIFORM METRES.

These have four lines, scanned alike, in each verse: one in general use, runs thus. There is no rhyme. The following metre, called Śārdūla, is in frequent use.

In the following instances, H. denotes the Hitopadeśa. R. the Raghu Vamśam. G.D. Ganga Das, whose rules are given in Dr. Yates' Sanskrit Grammar.

– – – ∪ ∪ – ∪ – ∪ ∪ ∪ – ‖ – – ∪ – – ∪ –

व्योमैका । न्तविहा । रिणोपि । विहगाः ‖ सम्प्राप्नु । वन्त्यापदं

H. i. 53.

vyōmai kān | tavihā | riṇōpi | vihagāḥ ‖ samprāpnu | vantyā padam

After the twelfth syllable there is cæsura, the harmonic pause: which in these pages will be marked ‖. This metre is very often used: In the Gīta Govinda there is an instance, in a song ending with these words:

कन्दर्पो पियमा यतेवि रचयन् ‖ शार्दूल विक्रीडि तं

Kandarpō | piyamā | yatēvi | rachayan ‖ Śārdūla | vikrīḍitam

The concluding words, "Śārdūla vikrīdita," give the name of the metre, which is also called Śārdūla.

Some metres have two pauses: Thus the मन्दाक्रान्ता Mandākrāntā: in which "The Cloud Messenger" is composed.

– – – – ‖ ∪ ∪ ∪ ∪ ∪ – ‖ – ∪ – – ∪ – –

मौनान् मूर्खः ‖ प्रवचनपटुर् ‖ वातुलो जल्पको वा

H. ii. 25.

Maunān mūrkhah ‖ pravachana paṭur ‖ vātulō jalpakō vā

The name is recollected by this line:

मन्दाक्रान्ता ‖ तदगुनियतं ‖ यक्षता ‖ मेतिबाला G.D.

"By slow and persevering efforts the maid is subdued."

This is one of the memorial lines framed by Ganga Dās; with Dr. Yates' translation: which I use throughout.

The Sragdhara metre also has two pauses

– – – – ∪ – – ‖ ∪ ∪ ∪ ∪ ∪ ∪ – ‖ – ∪ – – ∪ – –

Instance, from the Sakuntalā, verse 7:

ग्रीवाभङ्गाभिरामं ‖ मुहुरनुपतति ‖ स्यन्दने दत्तदृष्टिः

Grīvā bhang ābhirāmam
muhur anupatati
syandanē datta dṛishṭih.

Four such lines make the stanza. The memorial line is

मूर्तिर्गोपस्त्रयिष्णो ‖ रवतु जगतिवः ‖ स्रग्धराहारिहारा G.D.

The Indra vajrā इन्द्रवज्रा is a short metre: of which the first syllable is long or short at pleasure; and therefore is marked *x*.

x – ∪ – – ∪ ‖ ∪ – ∪ – –

गुणागुणज्ञा ‖ गुणिनो भवन्ति
तेनिर्गुणं प्रा ‖ प्यभवन्तिदोषाः H. i. 47.

Here the first syllable in the first line is short: in the second it is long.

In his notes on the Hitopadeśa, p. 280, Professor Johnson remarks that, "although not enjoined by a rule of prosody, a slight cæsura may often conveniently be made at the close of the fifth syllable." The cæsura is of importance to composers, but the reader may safely neglect it. The Sanskrit writers on prosody divide every line of the Uniform metres into threes, disregarding harmony.

Horace uses a similar metre. "Trahuntque siccas machinæ carinas."

More than a hundred Uniform metres are described: but not fifty are in use: and the few described in the next pages are all that the learner requires. For the present he may pass them by unread, and proceed to the Áryá.

The last syllable in each line by rule should be long: in practice it is free: either long or short at pleasure. The feet are,

– – ⏑ – – ‖ ⏑ ⏑ – ⏑ – –

Or if the initial is short,

⏑ – ⏑ – – ‖ ⏑ ⏑ – ⏑ – –

अर्थागमो नि ॥ त्यमरोगिता च
प्रिया च भार्या ॥ प्रियवादिनी च H. Introd. 19.

In the first line of this instance the initial syllable is long "artha:" in the second, "prĭ-yā," it is short.

If the first syllable is short it is called Upendra Vajrā: if the two are mingled, as they usually are, this is called आख्यानकी. But these names are needless. The one original name is enough: the others are not in use. Instances: H. Introd.

19, 25, 47. Book i. 27, 80, 114, etc., and R. ii. 1-74; v. 1-62, etc.

The Rāthōddhatā रथोद्धता ‾U‾ UUU ‖ ‾U‾ U‾

विग्रहः करितुरङ्गपत्तिभि

र्नोकदापि भवतां महीभृताम् H. iii. 153.

In this instance the two lines forming the couplet run into one another. Instances: R. ix. 68; xi. 1-91; xix. 1-55.

The mark [is a sign that this metre is unusual.

[Swāgatā स्वागता ‾U‾ UUU‾ UU‾‾

कुम्भपू रणभवः पटुर च्चै

रुच्चचारनिनदो ऽम्भसितस्याः R. ix. 73.

[Śālinī शालिनी ‾‾ ‾‾ ‾U‾ ‖ ‾U‾ ‾

निर्घातोग्रैः कुञ्जलीनां ‖ जिघांसु

र्ज्यानिर्घोषैः क्षोभया ‖ मास सिंहान् R. ix. 64.

XII Syllables.

The Vamśasthavila वंशस्थविल U‾U ‾‾U U‾U ‾U‾

नधर्मशास्त्रं ‖ पठतीतिकारणं H. i. ver. 16, 21, 115, 161, etc.

The Druta Vilambita द्रुतविलम्बित UUU ‾UU ‾UU ‾U‾

विपदि धैर्यमथाभ्युदये क्षमा

सदसि वाक्पटुता युधिविक्रमः H. i. 32.

Also 52. Suhrid. 71.

[Totaka तोटक UU‾ UU‾ UU‾ UU‾

सततिविनेतुरुदारमतेः R. viii. 90.

XIII Syllables.

[Manjubhāshiṇī मञ्जुभाषिणी

∪∪– ∪–∪ ∪∪ ॥ –∪– ∪–

इति विस्मृतान्यकर ॥ णीयमात्मनः R. ix. 69.

[Praharshiṇī प्रहर्षिणी ––– ∪∪∪∪ –∪– ∪––

निर्दिष्टां कुलपतिना स पर्णशालां R. i. 95.

See R. iv. 87, 88; viii. 91, etc.

Matta mayūra मत्तमयूर –– –– –∪∪ ––∪∪ ––

हातातेति क्रन्दितमाकर्ण्य विषण्ण-
स्तस्यान्विष्यन्वेतसगूढप्रभवंसः R. ix. 75.

XIV Syllables.

Vasanta tilakam वसन्ततिलका

––∪ –∪ ∪∪– ॥ ∪∪– ∪––

उद्योगिनं पुरुषसिंहमुपैतिलक्ष्मी
दैवेनदेयमितिकापुरुषावदन्ति H. Introd. 31.

See H. i, ver. 41, 83, 137, etc. R. Book v. 63-73, etc.

XV Syllables.

Mālinī मालिनी ∪∪∪ ∪∪∪ –– ॥ –∪– –∪– –

सलिलगगनविहारी कल्मषध्वंसकारी H. i. 20.

See H. i. 218. R. ii. 75; v. 74, 75, etc.

XVII Syllables.

Śikhariṇī शिखरिणी

∪––– –– ॥ ∪∪∪ ∪∪– ॥ –∪∪ ∪–

वरंमौनंकार्यं नच वचनमुक्तं यदनृतं H. i. 145.

See H. 145, 146, 187, etc.

Mandākrāntā मन्दाक्रान्ता

—— —— ‖ ∪∪∪ ∪∪— ‖ —∪— —∪— —

मौनान्मूर्खः ‖ प्रवचनपटु ‖ र्वातुलो जल्पको वा   H. ii. 25.

See ver. 160. R. viii. 94; xiv. 87, etc.

The Megha Duta is written in this metre.

Hariṇī हरिणी

∪∪∪ ∪∪— —— ‖ —— ∪— ‖ ∪∪— ∪— Or thus

∪∪∪ ∪∪— ‖ —— —— ‖ ∪— ∪∪— ∪—

सरसि बकशस् ‖ ताराच्छाये ‖ चयात् परिवञ्जितः

H. iv. 106. R. iii. 70.

Prithvī bharam पृथ्वीभरं

∪—∪ ∪∪— ∪— ‖ ∪∪∪ — ∪—— ∪—

जरस्य वदितं छतं ‖ शवशरीरमुद्वर्तितं

H. Notes, p. 108.

XVIII Syllables.

[Mahāmalikā: or, Nārācha; or, Lalā, or Vanamālā.

∪∪∪ ∪∪∪ —∪— —∪— —∪— —∪—

रघुपति रपि जातवेदोविशुद्धां प्रगृह्य प्रियां   R. xii. 104.

Charcharī चर्चरी

∪∪— ∪∪ ‖ ∪∪— ∪∪ ‖ ∪∪— ∪∪ ‖ ∪∪—

The following hymn to Ananga is quoted from the Siva-karṇ-āmritam, in the Śāradā tilakam.

शरणागत ‖ भरणातत ‖ करुणाकरहृदयं
सुरमानित परमाच्युत शरमारित विमतं
शमलाभित कमलासन विमलासन विनुतं
भजमानस निजमाश्रयम् अजमाहृत मदनम्

XIX Syllables.

Śārdula. This has already been explained. This name is noticed in Colebrooke: but he gives the same title to a different metre, of eighteen syllables (m s j s r m).

XXI Syllables.

The Sragdhara. This has already been explained.

XXV Syllables.

[The Krōncha-pada.

¯∪∪ ¯¯ ‖ ¯∪∪ ¯¯ ‖ ∪∪∪∪ ∪∪∪∪ ‖ ∪∪∪∪ ∪∪¯

क्रौञ्चपदाली चित्रततीरा मदकल खगकुल कलकल रुचिरा G.D.

The native prosodians scan all metres by trisyllabic feet: and this one, like the Sragdhara, is fancied intricate because such scansion does not agree with the melody: but if divided as here shown, it is clear. This metre is the basis of the पञ्झटिका, which will presently be noticed.

ALTERNATE UNIFORM METRE.

Musical time is called Tāla ताल: the "pollicis ictus," as Horace calls it: hence the name Vaitālīya. The eighth canto of the Raghu Vamsa begins thus.

अथतस्य वि ‖ वाहकौतुकं ∪∪¯ ∪∪ ‖ ¯∪¯ ∪¯

ललितं बिभ्रत ‖ एवपार्थिवः ∪∪¯ ¯∪∪ ‖ ¯∪¯ ∪¯

atha tas | ya vi | vāha kau | tukam
lalitam bibhrata | ēva pārthivah

The alternate lines have one long syllable inserted after the third. Each stanza has two such couplets. See Hitopad. Suhridb. 33, 85, 86. Sandhi, 101.

If a long syllable is added, the metre is called Aupachchhandasika औपच्छन्दसिक or 'A Variation.' Thus, Raghu Vamsa, ix. 66,

घमरागपरि ॥ तःप्रतितान्त्रः   UU¯ UU ‖ ¯U¯ U¯¯
क्वचिदाकर्णवि ॥ क्षष्टमक्षवर्षी   UU¯ ¯UU ‖ ¯U¯ U¯¯

This is used in the last canto of the Māgham, where the commentator observes "Sargēsmin Aupachchhandasikam vṛittam; Vaitālīyē gurv ādhikyat" सर्गेस्मिन्नौपच्छन्दसिकं वृत्तं वैतालीयेगुर्वाधिक्यात् "In this canto the metre is (Aupachchhandasikam) a variation, being the Vaitālīyam with an additional long syllable."

A variety of this is called Pushpitāgrā पुष्पिताग्रा (Hitop. Suhrid. 42).

अहितहितवि ॥ चारशून्यबुद्धेः
श्रुतिविषयी कैङ्क ॥ भि र्वेहिष्कृतस्य
UUU UUU ‖ ¯U¯ U¯¯
UUU UUUU ‖ ¯U¯ U¯¯

See also Hitop. Vigraha 145. Sakuntala, i. 32.

In all these metres the slōk has two similar lines: of which I cite the first alone. The final syllable of each couplet is long by rule: but in practice is often short, as here exhibited.

The alternate metres are popular: as Wilson observes (in his Grammar, p. 447) entire cantos of these occur in the Māgha, Kirātārjunīya, and Naishadha.

There are some varieties of the Vaitālīya: one is called Apara vaktra: thus defined by Colebrooke, citing R. ix. 70 (p. 124 in vol. ii. of his Essays). "Both verses are (*i.e.* each half is) terminated by three Iambicks: and begin with four short syllables: but one verse interposes a single short syllable, and the other a trochee." That is

∪∪∪∪   } ∪∪– ∪– ∪–
∪∪∪∪ – }

स्फुटसुमधुरवेणु गीतिभि
स्तमपरवक्त्रमवेत्यमाधवं G.D.

One variety of Vaitālīya, called Pravrĭttaca, runs thus:

In the first and third lines ∪– ∪∪∪ –∪– ∪–
In the second and fourth –∪– ∪∪∪ –∪– ∪–

The even lines prefix a long syllable: and may be expressed thus,

Lines 1 and 3   ∪– } ∪∪∪ –∪– ∪–
  „   2 and 4 –∪– }

The following instance is given by Colebrooke (p. 79),

इदं भरतवंशभूभृतां
श्रूयतां श्रुतिमनो रसायनं
पवित्रमधिकाशुभोदयं
व्यास वक्त्रकथितंप्रवृत्तकं

"Listen to this pure auspicious and pleasing history of the race of Bharata, as uttered from the mouth of Vyāsa."

The notes appended by Mr. Colebrooke, in pp. 79 and 155, may require a little explanation: but these refinements are needless to learners.

The alternate lines are called by different names. The uneven lines (1 and 3) are called Udīchya. The second and fourth, which are longer by one syllable, are named Prāchya. A stanza having four Udīchya lines is called Chāru hāsinī. One composed of four Prāchyas is named Aparāntikā.

THE A'RYA' आर्य्या.

The A'ryá uses feet that contain four breves, or the equivalents: having a long syllable in the

1st seat	– ⏑ ⏑
2nd „	⏑ – ⏑
3rd „	⏑ ⏑ –
Both long	– –
Four short	⏑ ⏑ ⏑ ⏑

Any one of these may be used in *even* seats, viz. 2, 4, 6. Each half must end in a long syllable: so it requires either – – the spondee, or ⏑ ⏑ – the anapæst. The following is in H. i. 33.

1 2 3
सम्पदि । यस्यन । हर्षो

4 5 6 7 8
विपदिवि । षादो । रणेच । धीर । त्वम्

1 2 3
– ⏑ ⏑   – ⏑ ⏑   – –

4 5 6 7 8
⏑ ⏑ ⏑ ⏑   – –   ⏑ – ⏑   – –   –

1 2 3
तंभुव । नत्रय । तिलकं

4 5 6 7 8
जनयति । जननी । सु । तंविर । लम्

1 2 3
– ⏑ ⏑   – ⏑ ⏑   ⏑ ⏑ –

4 5 6 7 8
⏑ ⏑ ⏑ ⏑   ⏑ ⏑ –   ⏑   – ⏑ ⏑   –

In the eighth seat (in this instance) each half has a long. In the sixth, the first half has an amphibrach: but the second has a single breve.

This is the usual mode: having variations in the sixth and

eighth places. But a kind called आर्य्या गीति āryā-gīti has those places otherwise: Kālidāsa's Nalōdaya has many instances: thus (canto ii. 41),

1 2 3
काषति रश्मिभि ताभिः

4 5 6 7 8
स्फुटमद् भिरियम् हिविहति रश्मिभि ताभिः

1 2 3
¯∪∪ ¯∪∪ ¯¯

4 5 6 7 8
∪∪¯ ∪∪¯ ∪∪∪∪ ¯∪∪ ¯¯

and the second half is constructed in the same manner.

The final syllable in each half, by rule is long: but in practice is often short.

The amphibrach Ja जगण is never used in the uneven seats: which are 1, 3, 5, 7. To aid the memory I express the rule thus:—"Aryæ sedibus imparibus prohibete Jajāpa." Here "aryæ" is a spondæus, as "aureā" in the Æneid i. 698, and vii. 190.

The sixth foot in each half is either NL ∪∪∪∪ or J ∪¯∪ or a single breve.

The few rules now given are sufficient to explain the Árya. The remaining observations, which native tutors consider essential, may be considered at leisure. A metre used by Horace is similar to the Árya.

Miserar' | est neq'a | mori
Dare lu | dum neque | dul | ci mala | vino
Lavere aut | exani | mari
Metuen | tes patru | æ | vulnera | linguæ

Tibi qua | lum Cytha | reæ
Puer a | les tibi | tē | las oper | osæ
que Miner | væ studi' | aufert
Neobu | le Lipa | ræ | i nitor | Hebri

⏑⏑– –⏑⏑ ––
⏑⏑– –⏑⏑ |–| –⏑⏑ ––
⏑⏑– –⏑⏑ ––
⏑⏑– –⏑⏑ |–| –⏑⏑ ––

Another Horatian metre is analogous: thus,

Sic te diva potens Cypri
Sic fra | tres Hele | næ | lucida | sidera, etc.

–– –⏑⏑ –⏑–
–– –⏑⏑ |–| –⏑⏑ –⏑⏑

But these are Uniform metres: whereas the A'ryá has many melodious variations. The following species, some of them mere matters of curiosity, are preserved in Yates' Grammar. The fanciful instances there copied from Gangā Dās, are various hymns, so contrived as to exhibit the name of the species. But I shall subjoin passages from popular poems.

The first, called पथ्या Pathyā, or ordinary, has already been explained.

2. Vipulā विपुला, a "broad or extensive" class, admitting several varieties. Some are composed entirely of breves, except of course the final syllables. This is called Nā-vipulā, because composed of (Na) tribachs. Some verses in the same A'ryá metre are written (excepting the sixth seat as usual) entirely in long syllables: this is called Mā-vipulā: because it may be measured by (molossi) feet of three longs: which of

course would seem against the prescribed principles: thus in the Sānkhyā Kārikā

Alpa grantham spashtam ‒‒ ‒‒ ‒‒

The name denotes the pause (see Colebrooke, p. 154), and if this is in the first half it is called "ādi vipulā;" if in the second "antya vipulā;" if in both, "ubhaya vipulā." Some of the learned consider this name, and "chapalā" *variable*, to have the same meaning. The Árya by rule admits only five sorts of feet: but the Vipulā rule admits nearly every variety consistent with the original principle.

The following instances are framed by Gangā Dās. The first is पथ्या and is thus exemplified.

कृष्णः । शिशुः सु । तोमे
वल्लव । कुलटा । भिराहू । तोमगृ । हे
क्षणमपि । वसत्य । सावित्ति
जगाद । गोप्यां । य । शोदा । ख्यां

‒‒ ∪‒∪ ‒‒
‒∪∪ ∪∪‒ ∪‒∪ ‒∪∪ ‒
∪∪∪∪ ∪‒∪ ‒∪∪
∪‒∪ ‒‒ ∪ ‒‒ ‒

"Krishna, this boy of mine, being called by the milkmaids, will not remain at home a single moment: thus said his venerable mother."

One variety runs thus:

वृन्दा । वनेस । लीलं
कल्प । द्रुमका । ण्डनिहित । तनुय । ष्टिः

खेरमु । खार्पित । वेणुः
कृष्णो । यदिमन । सि । कःस्व । र्गः

−− ∪−∪ −−
−− ∪∪− ∪∪∪∪ ∪∪− −
−∪∪ −∪∪ −−
−− ∪∪∪∪ ।∪। −− −

"If Krishna, reclining negligently against a tree in the Vrinda wood, and playing his flute with a smiling face, remains in the mind, then what is heaven?"

The next three instances point to a matter of mere curiosity. It is regarding the use of the amphibrachys (Ja) in the fourth seat. In H. ii. 5

आलस्यं स्त्रीसेवा । सरोग

ālas | yam strī | sēvā | sărōgă

Here the fourth foot of the first half has (Ja) the amphibrachys sărōga: the same occurs in verses 161, 162 and elsewhere. This is called मुखचपला Mukha chapalā, or "Καλλιοπη."

But this may occur in the second half, and then is named जघनचपला Jaghana chapalā or "Καλλιπυγη." So in H. ii. 74 the second half has

प्राप्यम गुण्यवि शेषं भवन्ति

Here is the amphibrachys in the fourth seat; "bhavanti."

But sometimes the amphibrachys occupies the fourth seat in each half. This is called उभयचपला Ubhaya chapalā: or Mahā chapalā (see Colebr. p. 154), or simply चपला chapalā. In Greek this might be styled αμφικαλη or περικαλη. Thus in the philosophical treatise Sānkhyā Kārikā, verse 61,

प्रकृतेः सुकुमारतरं नकिंचिदस्तीति मेमतिर्भवति
या दृष्टा स्मीति पुनर्नदर्शनमुपैतिपुरुषस्य

Prakriteh | sukumā | rataram
Nākimchi, etc.
Yā drisht | āsmī | ti punar
Nă dārshă, etc.

"Nothing, in my opinion, is more gentle than nature: once aware of having been seen, she does not again expose herself to the gaze of soul." (Colebrooke.)

These instances of Chapalā may be passed over by the learner, being of no importance.

ON RHYMING METRES.

A few metres use a closing rhyme, connecting two lines into one couplet. One is called Prajjaṭika प्रज्झटिका or Manjarī मंजरी. It is similar to the Kronchapada, already described: but that is uniform, whereas the Manjarī admits feet equivalent to a spondee, being nearly the same as those used in the Áryá: excepting ∪–∪ (Jaganam), and the feet used are,

–∪∪	B	having a long in the first place.
∪∪–	S	in the third.
––	Gā,	the spondee.
∪∪∪∪	NL	four shorts.

The last syllable in each line is long.

Mūdha ja | hīhi dhan | āgama | trishńam
Kuru tanu | buddhi ma | nah suvi | trishńam

–∪∪ –∪∪ –∪∪ ––
∪∪∪∪ –∪∪ –∪∪ ––

The Mugdha-bōdha or Mallet of Delusion, a popular carol

attributed to the ancient sage Sankarachārya, was first printed by Sir William Jones, who remarks that "it is composed in regular anapæstic verses according to the strictest rules of Greek prosody." But he gives no analysis of the metre, and none can be found in any published volume. Yet those who have listened to the verse as chanted by learned Brahmans will perceive that the definition I have given is correct.

मोहमुद्गरः

1. मूढ ज। हीहि ध। नागम। तृष्णां   —◡◡ —◡◡ —◡◡ ——
कुरु तनु। बुद्धिम। नःसु वि। तृष्णां। ◡◡◡◡ —◡◡ —◡◡ ——
यल्लभ। से निज। कर्मो। पात्तं   —◡◡ —◡◡ —— ——
वित्तं। तेन वि। नोदय। चित्तं ॥   —— —◡◡ —◡◡ ——

2. का तव। कान्ता। कस्ते। पुत्रः   —◡◡ —— —— ——
संसा। रो ऽयम। तीव वि। चित्रः   —— —◡◡ —◡◡ ——
कस्य। त्वं वा। कुत आ। यातः   —— —— ◡◡— ——
तत्त्वं। चिन्तय। तदिदं। भ्रातः ॥   —— —◡◡ ◡◡— ——

3. मा कुरु। धनजन। यौवन। गर्वं   —◡◡ ◡◡◡◡ —◡◡ ——
हरति नि। मेषा। त्कालः। सर्वं।   ◡◡◡◡ —— —— ——
माया। मयमिद्। मखिलं। हित्वा   —— ◡◡◡◡ ◡◡— ——
ब्रह्मप। दं प्रवि। शाशु वि। दित्वा ॥ —◡◡ —◡◡ —◡◡ ——

4. नलिनी। दलगत। जलव। त्तरलं   ◡◡— ◡◡◡◡ ◡◡— ◡◡—
तद्व। ज्जीवन। मतिशय। चपलं   —— —◡◡ ◡◡◡◡ ◡◡—
क्षणमिह। सज्जन। संगति। रेका   ◡◡◡◡ —◡◡ —◡◡ ——
भवति भ। वार्णव। तरणे। नौका ॥ ◡◡◡◡ —◡◡ ◡◡— ——

5. याव। ज्जननं। ताव। न्मरणं	——	⏑⏑—	——	⏑⏑—
ताव। ज्जननी। जठरे। शयनं।	——	⏑⏑—	⏑⏑—	⏑⏑—
इति सं। सारे। स्फुटतर। दोषः	⏑⏑—	——	⏑⏑⏑⏑	——
कथमिह। मानव तव संतोषः॥	⏑⏑⏑⏑	—⏑⏑	⏑⏑—	——
6. दिनया। मिन्यौ। सायं। प्रातः	⏑⏑—	——	——	——
शिशिरव। सन्ती पुनरा। यातः।	⏑⏑⏑⏑	——	⏑⏑—	——
कालः। क्रीडति। गच्छ। त्यायुः	——	—⏑⏑	——	——
तदपि न। मुञ्च। त्याशा। वायुः॥	⏑⏑⏑⏑	——	——	——
7. अङ्गं। गलितं। पलितं। मुण्डं	——	⏑⏑—	⏑⏑—	——
दन्तवि। हीनं। यातं। तुण्डं।	—⏑⏑	——	——	——
करधृत। कम्पित। शोभित। दण्डं	⏑⏑⏑⏑	—⏑⏑	—⏑⏑	——
तदपि न। मुञ्च। त्याशाभाण्डं॥	⏑⏑⏑⏑	——	——	——
8. सुरवर। मन्दिर। तरुतल। वासः	⏑⏑⏑⏑	—⏑⏑	⏑⏑⏑⏑	——
शय्या। भूतल। मजिनं। वासः।	——	—⏑⏑	⏑⏑—	——
सर्वप। रिग्रह। भोग। त्यागः	—⏑⏑	—⏑⏑	——	——
कस्य सु। खं न क। रोति वि। रागः॥	—⏑⏑	—⏑⏑	—⏑⏑	——
9. शत्रौ। मित्रे। पुत्रे। बन्धौ	——	——	——	——
मा कुरु। यत्नं। विग्रह। सन्धौ।	—⏑⏑	——	—⏑⏑	——
भव सम। चित्तः सर्व। त्र त्वं	⏑⏑⏑⏑	——	——	——
वाञ्छ। स्यचिरा। द्यदि विष्णुत्वं	——	⏑⏑—	⏑⏑—	——
10. अष्टकु। लाचल। सप्तस। मुद्रा	—⏑⏑	—⏑⏑	—⏑⏑	——
ब्रह्मपु। रन्दर। दिनकर। रुद्राः।	—⏑⏑	—⏑⏑	⏑⏑⏑⏑	——
न त्वं। नाहं। नायं। लोकः	——	——	——	——
तदपि कि। मर्थं। क्रियते। शोकः॥	⏑⏑⏑⏑	——	⏑⏑—	——

11. त्वयि मयि। चान्य। त्रैको विष्णुः	◡◡◡◡	—	—	—
व्यर्थं। कुप्यसि। मय्यस। हिष्णुः।	—	—◡◡	—◡◡	—
सर्वं। पश्या। त्मन्या। त्मानं	—	—	—	—
सर्व। त्रोत्सृज। भेद। ज्ञानं॥	—	—◡◡	—	—
12. बाल। स्ताव। त्क्रीडा। सक्तः	—	—	—	—
तरुण। स्ताव। त्तरुणी। रक्तः।	◡◡—	—	◡◡—	—
वृद्ध। स्ताव। च्चिन्ता। मग्नः	—	—	—	—
परमे। ब्रह्मणि। को पि न। लग्नः॥	◡◡—	—◡◡	—◡◡	—
13. द्वादश। पञ्जटि। काभिर। शेषः	—◡◡	—◡◡	—◡◡	—
शिष्या। णां कथि। तो ह्युप। देशः।	—	—◡◡	—◡◡	—
येषां। नैष क। रोति वि। वेकं	—	—◡◡	—◡◡	—
तेषां। कः कुरु। तामति। रेकं॥	—	—◡◡	—◡◡	—

TRANSLATION, BY SIR WILLIAM JONES.

The Mallet of Delusion.

1. Restrain, deluded mortal, thy thirst of acquiring wealth; excite an aversion from it in thy body, understanding, and inclination: with the riches which thou acquirest by thine own actions, with these satisfy thy soul.

2. Who is thy wife, who thy son; how extremely wonderful is even this world; whose *creature* thou also *art*; whence thou camest; meditate on this, o brother, *and again* on this.

3. Make no boast of opulence, attendants, youth; all these time snatches away in the twinkling of an eye: checking all this illusion like Maya, set thy heart on the foot of Brahme, speedily gaining knowledge of Him.

4. As a drop of water moves tremulous on the lotos-leaf, thus is human life inexpressibly slippery: the company of the virtuous *endures* here but for a moment; that is our ship in passing the ocean of the world.

5. The body is tottering; the head grey; the mouth toothless: the delicate staff trembles in the hand which holds it: still the flagon of covetousness remains unemptied.

6. How soon are we born! how soon dead! how long lying in the mother's womb! how great is the prevalence of vice in this world! Wherefore o man hast thou complacency here below?

7. Day and night, evening and morning, winter and spring, depart and return: time sports, life passes on; yet the wind of expectation continues unrestrained.

8. To dwell under the mansion of the high gods at the foot of a tree, to have the ground for a couch, and a hide for vesture; to renounce all extrinsic enjoyments; whom doth not such devotion fill with delight?

9. Place not thy affections too strongly on foe or friend, on a son or a kinsman; in war or peace; be thou even-minded towards all, if thou desirest speedily to attain the nature of Vishnu.

10. The Eight great mountains, the seven seas, Brahme, Indra, the Sun, and Rudra, *these are permanent:* not thou, nor I, nor this or that people: wherefore then should anxiety be raised *in our minds?*

11. In thee, in me, in every other being is Vishnu; foolishly art thou offended with me, not bearing my approach: see every soul in thine own soul; in all places lay aside a notion of diversity.

12. The boy so long delights in his play; the youth so long pursues his damsel; the old man so long broods over uneasiness, that no one meditates on the Supreme Being.

13. This is the instruction of learners delivered in twelve distinct stanzas; what more can be done with such as this work fills not with devotion.

Another instance is given of this metre. It is said that a serpent lodged in a dry tree was described in a dry verse by a Vedānti,

शुष्को । वृक्ष । स्तिष्ठ । त्यग्रे   – –   – –   – –   – –

तदुपरि । सर्प । स्तिष्ठति   ∪∪∪∪   – –   – ∪∪

for which Kālidāsa proposed, extempore, in the same metre,

नीरस । तरुरिह निवसति निकटे   –∪∪ ∪∪∪∪ ∪∪∪∪ ∪∪–
कोटर । मध्ये । कुटिलभु । जङ्गः   –∪∪ – – ∪∪∪∪ – –

The Moha Mudgara was printed in the Telugu character at Madras in 1865: and to it is subjoined a continuation in fifteen stanzas, beginning thus,

काते । कान्ता । धनगत । चिंता
वातुल । किंतव । नास्तिनि । यन्ता
त्रिजगति । सज्जन । सङ्गति । रेका
भवतिभ । वार्णव । तरणे । नौका

There are some popular melodies unnoticed in the treatises on Prosody. In the twenty-first canto of the tenth book of the Srī Bhāgavat there are a set of गोपिकागीत Milkmaids' Carols, which are usually considered musical, free from prosodial rule. But we shall find they are regular, allowing of a variation in the beginning of a line. The final syllable is free.

∪∪∪ }
–∪ } –∪– –∪– ∪–

जयति । तेधिकं । जन्मना । व्रज
श्श्रयत । इन्दिरा । शश्वद । त्रहि ।
दयित । दृश्यता । न्दिक्षुता । वका
स्त्वयि धृ । तासव । स्त्वांवि । चिन्वते etc., etc.

This metre is not explained in the Manjari; nor by Ganga Dās, Colebrooke, Yates, or even in Weber (p. 371-377), where he describes the eleventh system.

Dandaka.

The Dandaka दण्डक is a chant, dithyrambic metre, or poetical prose: having the feet ‒ ‒ ⏑ ‒ ‒ ⏑ two long syllables followed by a breve, or as some express it ⏑ ‒ ‒ ⏑ ‒ ‒ which is the same. It is of unlimited length: and in printing it may be conveniently divided into lines having four or five feet in each. It usually commences with ⏑⏑⏑ ⏑⏑⏑ ⏑ ‒ ⏑. At the close one or two longs may be added. The native treatises as usual give numerical rules, which Colebrooke records. The instance he adduces (p. 144) runs thus,

⏑⏑⏑⏑ ⏑⏑ ‒ ⏑ । ‒ ‒ ⏑ । ‒ ‒ ⏑ । ‒ ‒ ⏑ etc.

प्रचलितकरिझम्पि । पर्यन्त । चंचम्न । खाघात etc.

Various names which he mentions, are given to various sorts: but what has now been stated will explain them all.

This is all the student requires regarding Sanskrit Prosody. No native tutor will teach it in this plain way: but I never met a single pandit who could expound all the metres given in these few pages.

APPENDIX.

As it is my object to simplify the Prosody, I have given only such rules as are in general use, and in the following pages such matters will be noticed as are valued by the learned, though of small utility to the learner. If at a future day he reads a native treatise on the subject, or Weber's German volume, he will find a wilderness of rules tending rather to impede than facilitate his progress.

The letters used as names of the prosodial feet were selected at an early age, and have been in use throughout India for three thousand years at least. They are combined in an ancient line, written by Pānini,

Ya mā tā rā ja bhā na sa la gam

यमाताराजभानसलगं

Each of these syllables is the name of a foot: and that syllable with the next two will exemplify the foot. Thus the first three are Yămātā, which is the foot Y. The next three Mātārā make the foot M. Then Tārāja are the foot T. Rājabha is R, while Jabhāna is J. Bhānasa is B, the dactyl. Nasala is N, the tribrach; and Salagam is S, the anapæst. The closing syllables are L for breve and G for a long.

Some other feet are known by names merely compounded from those already given.

GREEK NAME.		SANSKRIT EXPRESSION.	INSTANCE.
Choriambus	–∪∪–	bha-gam	ebrietas
Antispastus	∪––∪	ya-lam	Alexander
Ionic à majore	––∪∪	ta-lam	producere
Ionic à minore	∪∪––	sa-gam	similes sint
Pæan I.	–∪∪∪	bha-lam	temporibus
„ II.	∪–∪∪	ja-lam	potentia
„ III.	∪∪–∪	sa-lam	animatus
„ IV.	∪∪∪–	na-gam	celeritas
Epitrite I.	∪–––	ya-gam	salutantes
„ II.	–∪––	ra-gam	concitati
„ III.	––∪–	ta-gam	communicans
„ IV.	–––∪	ma-lam	incantare
Proceleusmatic	∪∪∪∪	na-lam	hominibus

The Tables of Uniform Metres given by Mr. Colebrooke and Dr. Yates are correct and valuable, but require some explanation. Being translated from native works they are rendered intricate with arithmetical contrivances apparently intended to involve the art in mystery. For instance, if we are searching for a definition of that familiar metre, the Śärdula, we first must count the syllables in one line: these being nineteen, we consult Yates, who places it (p. 370) under the "Nineteenth Genus" as "Species 3rd." But he omits the names. To find the name we must turn to p. 246, where, at "XIX," is given the name of the Genus "Atidhriti;" and here, at No. 3, we discover the name sought.

Mr. Colebrooke, always exact, but not always clear, makes the matter more intricate (in p. 163) by changing the numeral, thus: instead of the xixth he marks the genus as xivth, and defines it "xiv Atidhriti, 19 × 4 = 76;" and here is the metre Śārdula, given as the *first* species: defined thus "Śārdūla vicrīditā, or Śárdúla (12 + 7) *m s j s* 2 *t g* = S D 2 T A + S I C." The numerals denote that there is a pause or cæsura after the twelfth syllable. The letters "*m s j s* 2 *t g*" denote the feet magaṇam, sagaṇam, etc., and the capitals S D, etc., give the initials of a spondee, a dactyl, and so on.

In translating Ganga Dās's prosody Dr. Yates has preserved the memorial lines, which are useful as recording the names. But another arrangement would be easier. Thus the ninth canto of the Raghu Vamsa opens with this metre,

⏑⏑⏑ –⏑⏑ –⏑⏑ –⏑– NBBR

To discover the name we must first count the syllables: as they are twelve, we turn to Yates, where, under the 12th Genus (p. 357) we find it as the 9th species. But to learn the name we must refer to p. 425, where, at xii. 9 is the "Druta Vilambita."

Stenzler, in his prosodial notes on the poem, follows the native routine, but using still further obscurity. Instead of stating that there are twelve syllables, he says "Jagati, sive disticha 48 sylls.," leaving the reader to guess that as there are forty-eight in the stanza there are twelve syllables in the line.

Jagati is merely a mysterious word for twelve. This and the other similar names are rarely remembered even by excellent pandits: and are of no use.

The names of the Chhands.

I	उक्था	XIV	शक्वरी
II	अत्युक्था	XV	अतिशक्वरी
III	मध्या	XVI	अष्टी
IV	प्रतिष्ठा	XVII	अत्यष्टी
V	सुप्रतिष्ठा	XVIII	धृति
VI	गायत्री	XIX	अतिधृति
VII	उष्णिह् (Nom. उष्णिक्)	XX	कृति
VIII	अनुष्टुभ् (Nom. अनुष्टुप्)	XXI	प्रकृति
IX	बृहती	XXII	आकृति
X	पंक्ति	XXIII	विकृति
XI	त्रिष्टुभ् (Nom. त्रिष्टुप)	XXIV	सत्कृति
XII	जगती	XXV	अतिकृति
XIII	अतिजगती	XXVI	उत्कृति

Metres of greater length are called दण्डक, musical prose, of which there are many varieties.

Dr. Rosen, the learned editor of Colebrooke, confessed to me that he had printed the tables without understanding them.

The metres mentioned as having less than eleven syllables are often portions of longer kinds. They are seen only in native books on prosody, and are of no advantage to the student.

The letters M, B, J, R, G, L, etc., denote the feet according to the ancient method.

XI. Verses having eleven syllables in each line.

1. इन्द्रवज्रा — — ∪ — — ‖ ∪ ∪ — ∪ — — 2 T J — —

Example given by G.D. गोष्ठेगिरिंसव्यक रेणधृत्वा। रुष्टेन्द्रवज्राहति-युक्तवृष्टौ Holding over them a mountain in his left hand.

2. उपेन्द्रवज्रा ∪–∪ –– ॥ ∪∪– ∪–– JTJ––

उपेन्द्रवज्रादिमणिच्छटाभिः Shining with the pearly brightness of thunderbolts, etc.

3. सुमुखी ∪∪∪ ∪–∪ ∪–∪ ∪– N2JLG

तिमिरमुदस्य मुखंसुमुखी She, beautiful, (beheld) his darkness-destroying face.

4. शालिनी ––– ––∪– –∪–– M2TGā

पुंसां श्रद्धाशालिनी विष्णुभक्तिः True faith in Vishṇu (promotes the holiness) of men.

5. वातोर्मी ––– –∪∪ ––∪ –– MBTGā

वातोर्म्मी पोत मिवाम्भो धिमध्ये As a raging wind destroys a boat in the midst of the sea.

6. भ्रमरविलसिता ––– –∪∪ ∪∪∪ ∪– MBNLG

फुल्लावल्ली भ्रमरविलसिता An expanded flower adorned with humming bees.

7. अनुकूला –∪∪ ––∪ ∪∪∪ –– BTNGā

स्यादनुकूलाजगतिनकस्य Is there any one in the world whose (wish) has not been granted?

8. रथोद्धता –∪– ∪∪∪ ॥ –∪– ∪– RNRLG

कृष्णवेणुनिनदैरथोद्धता She was startled at the sound of Krishṇa's flute.

9. स्वागता –∪– ∪∪∪ । –∪∪ –– RNBGā

स्वागतादरकरः सुरवर्गः All the gods respect him.

10. दोधक –∪∪ –∪∪ । –∪∪ –– 3BGā

देवसदो धकदम्बतलस्थः Placed at the foot of the Kadamba tree, under which the gods assemble.

11. मोटनक ––⏑ ⏑–⏑ ⏑–⏑ ⏑– T2JLG

चाणूरमहा भटमोटनकं The destruction of the great armies of the infernals.

12. श्येनी –⏑– ⏑–⏑ –⏑– ⏑– TJTLG

श्येन्यशेषलोकपावनी सदा White and constantly purifying all people.

XII.

1. चन्द्रवर्त्म –⏑– ⏑⏑⏑ –⏑⏑ ⏑⏑– RNBS

चन्द्रवर्त्म निहितं घनतिमिरैः The path of the moon is obstructed by thick darkness.

2. वंशस्थविल ⏑–⏑ ––⏑ ⏑–⏑ –⏑– JTJR

विलासवंशस्थविलं मुखा निलैः The sweet-toned flute (was filled) by the breeze of his lips.

A grammarian has here remarked that the metre commonly employed in Greek Tragedies much resembles this "twelfth class." But the tragic metres are variable, while those in the Sanskrit system are Uniform.

3. जलोद्धतगति ⏑–⏑ ⏑⏑– ⏑–⏑ ⏑⏑– JSJS

कलिन्दतनयाजलोद्धतगतिः The swelling motion of the waters of the Yamunā.

4. भुजङ्गप्रयात ⏑–– ⏑–– ⏑–– ⏑–– 4Y

भुजङ्गप्रयातं द्रुतंसागराय O Serpent! (make) your departure quickly to the sea.

5. तोटक ⏑⏑– ⏑⏑– ⏑⏑– ⏑⏑– 4S

मुदितोऽटकलेरपनेतुमघं Go, happy to obtain freedom from sin in the iron age.

6. स्रग्विणी –⏑– –⏑– –⏑– –⏑– 4R

मूर्तिरास्तां ममैवोरसि स्रग्विणी May his form be a bracelet in my bosom.

7\. वैश्वदेवी ––– ––– U–– U–– 2M2Y

भ्रातः सम्पन्ना राधना वैश्वदेवी O brother! every goddess will be worshipped.

8\. प्रमिताक्षरा UU– U–U UU– UU– SJ2S

प्रमिताक्षरा मुररिपोर्भणितिः The melodious sounds of Krishṇa's voice.

9\. द्रुतविलम्बित UUU –UU –UU –U– N2BR

द्रुतविलम्बितचारुविहारिणं Enchanting by his swift, slow and delightful paces.

10\. मन्दाकिनी UUU UUU –U– –U– 2N2R

पदजलरुहि यस्य मन्दाकिनी From whose lotos-feet the Mandākinī sprung.

11\. विचित्रा UUU U–– UUU U–– NYNS

विपिनविहारेकुसुमविचित्रा (His form) is adorned with flowers when he wanders in the grove.

12\. तामरस UUU U–U U–U U–– N2JY

तवमुखतामरसं मुरशत्रो Thy lotos face, o enemy of Mura.

13\. मालती UUU U–U U–U –U– N2JR

अलिरपि चुम्बति मालतीं मुहुः And the bee is constantly embracing the flower.

14\. मणिमाला ––U U–– ––U U–– TYTY

जातप्रतिबिम्बा शोणामणिमाला An image like a chaplet of red pearls.

15\. जलधरमाला –––– UUUU –––– MGNLMG

तापोच्छेदे जलधरमालानव्या New clouds for the destroying of heat.

XIII.

1\. प्रहर्षिणी ––– UUU U–U –U–– MNJRG

संसारे मतिरभवत्प्रहर्षिणीह In the world he was delighted.

2. रुचिरा, or, प्रभावती ∪–∪ –∪∪ ∪∪– ∪–∪– JBSJG

परिभ्रमन् व्रजरुचिराङ्गनान्तरे Wandering among the beautiful women of Vraja.

3. मत्तमयूर ––– ––∪ ∪–– ∪∪–– MTYSG

लीलानृत्यं मत्तमयूरध्वनिकान्तं Rendered vocal by the noise of peacocks full of play.

4. चण्डी ∪∪∪ ∪∪∪ ∪∪– ∪∪– ∪ 2N2SG

चरणकमलयुगचापलचण्डी Terrible in the dance of his lotos-like feet.

5. मंजुभाषिणी ∪∪– ∪–∪ ∪∪– ∪–∪– SJSJG

मुदमच्युते व्यधितमंजुभाषिणी She, speaking pleasantly promotes the joy of the imperishable one.

6. चन्द्रिका ∪∪∪ ∪∪∪ ––∪ ––∪ – 2N2SG

शरदमृतरुचचन्द्रिकाचालिते Enjoying the autumnal rains (by the side of a river) irradiated by the light of the moon.

7. कलहंस, or, सिंहनाद

∪∪– ∪–∪ ∪∪– ∪∪– – SJ2SJG

यमुनाविहारकुतुककलहंसः A drake in the pleasant parts of the Yamunā.

8. प्रबोधिता ∪∪– ∪–∪ ∪∪– ∪–∪ – SJSJG

स्मितमाततान सपदिप्रबोधिता Being awaked at that time she smiled.

9. मृगेन्द्रमुख ∪∪∪ ∪–∪ ∪–∪ –∪– – N2JRG

क्षुधितमृगेन्द्रमुखंमृगा उपेत्य A deer falling into the mouth of a hungry lion.

XIV.

1. असंबाधा ––– –– ∪∪∪ ∪∪∪ ––– MGā2NM

साधूनांबाधां प्रशमयतु स कंसारिः May the foe of Kamsā assuage the afflictions of the virtuous.

2. वसंततिलक ‒ ‒ ∪ ‒ ∪ ∪ ∪ ‒ ∪ ∪ ‒ ∪ ‒ ‒ SB2JGā

फुल्लं वसन्ततिलकं तिलकं वनाल्याः The tila plant and the glory of the groves is full blown.

3. अपराजिता ∪ ∪ ∪ ∪ ∪ ∪ ‒ ∪ ‒ ∪ ∪ ‒ ∪ ‒ 2NRSLG

यदुजचमूः परैरपराजिता The army under the command of the son of Yadu was invincible.

4. प्रहरण कलिका

∪ ∪ ∪ ∪ ∪ ∪ ‒ ∪ ∪ ∪ ∪ ∪ ∪ ‒ 2NBNLG

व्यथयति कुसुमप्रहरणकलिका O Cupid! thy flow'ry arrow gives great pain.

5. वासन्ती

‒ ‒ ‒ ‒ ‒ ∪ ∪ ∪ ∪ ‒ ‒ ‒ ‒ ‒ MTNMGā

कंसारातौ नृत्यति सदृशी वासन्तीयं When the destroyer of Kamsa dances he resembles the Vāsanta tree.

6. लोला ‒ ‒ ‒ ∪ ∪ ‒ ‒ ‒ ‒ ‒ ∪ ∪ ‒ ‒ MSMBGā

मुग्धे यौवनलक्ष्मीर्विद्युद्विभ्रमलोला O fair one, the glory of youth is transient as a flash of lightning.

7. नान्दीमुखी ∪ ∪ ∪ ∪ ∪ ∪ ‒ ‒ ∪ ‒ ‒ ∪ ‒ ‒ 2N2TGā

सरसखगकुलालापनान्दीमुखीयं It's surface is rendered vocal by the chirping of birds.

XV.

1. शशिकला, or, शशिलेखा

∪ ∪ ∪ ∪ ∪ ∪ ∪ ∪ ∪ ∪ ∪ ∪ ∪ ∪ ‒ 4NS

मलयजतिलकसमुद्रितशशिकला The crescent painted (on his forehead) with sandal paste.

2. मालिनी

∪ ∪ ∪ ∪ ∪ ∪ ‒ ‒ ॥ ‒ ∪ ‒ ‒ ∪ ‒ ‒ 2NGā ॥ G2Y

धृतमधुरिपुलीला मालिनी पातु राधा May Rādhā who assumed the colour of Madhu's destroyer grant protection.

3. लीलाखेल — — — — — — — — — — — — — — — 5 M

रासोल्लासक्रीडद्गोपीभिः सार्धं लीलाखेलः Full of play with the sprightly playful milkmaids.

4. विपिनतिलक

∪∪∪ ∪∪— ∪∪∪ —∪— —∪— NSN2R

विपिनतिलकं विकसितं वसन्तागमे The tila plant is in full bloom in the opening of spring.

5. तूणक —∪ —∪ —∪ —∪ ‖ —∪ —∪ —∪ —

RJRJR 7 trochees and a long.

पंचबाणबाणजालपूर्णहेमतूणकं A golden quiver full of Cupid's arrows.

6. चन्द्रलेखा

— — — —∪— — — — ∪— — ∪— — MRM2Y

राधाम्भोदस्य गर्भे लीना यथा चन्द्रलेखा Rādhā was like the moon shining a little through a dark cloud.

7. चित्रा — — — — — — — — — ∪— — ∪— — 3M2Y

खेलन्मुक्ता हारावन्यस्रग्ल सत्वर्दचित्रा His form is ornamented with a necklace of wild flowers, resembling one of bright pearls.

XVI.

1. चित्र, or चित्रसंग, or चंचला, double Samānica (says Colebr.)

—∪— ∪—∪ —∪— ∪—∪ —∪— ∪ 8 trochees

त्वां सदैव वासुदेव पुण्यलभ्यपादसेव । वन्यपुष्प चित्रकेश संस्मरामि गोपवेश (In this metre each line ends in a breve). I muse on thee, o Vishṇu, the worship of whose feet imparts virtue, having thy tresses wreathed with wild flowers, disguised as a cowherd.

2. गजविलसित

—∪∪ —∪— ∪∪∪ ∪∪∪ ∪∪∪ — BR3NG

कंसनिदेशदृप्यदृ षभगजविलसितं The prancing of the huge elephant ruled by Kamsa.

3. चकिता

¯UU UU¯ ¯¯¯ ¯¯U UUU ¯ BSMTNG

दुर्जयदनुज श्रेणी दुश्चेष्टाश्रुत चकिता (The earth) was terrified at the wicked pursuits of the almost invincible giants.

4. विचित्र, or, पञ्चचामर

8 iambicks U¯ U¯ U¯ U¯ ॥ U¯ U¯ U¯ U¯

सुरद्रुमूलमण्डपेवि ॥ चित्ररत्न निर्मिते He dwells in a house made of shining pearls, at the root of a celestial tree.

5. मदनललित

¯¯¯ ¯UU UUU ¯¯¯ UUU ¯ MBNMNG

राधात्यर्थंमदनललितान्दोले ऽलसवपु: Rādhā is languishing on the swing (balancing doubt) of love.

6. वाणि UUU ¯U¯ ¯UU U¯U ¯U¯ ¯ NRBJRG

स्फुरतुममानने ऽप्यनणुवाणिरीतिरम्यं May the goddess of speech now inspire in me the graces of poetry.

7. प्रवरललित

U¯¯ ¯¯¯ UUU UU¯ ¯U¯ ¯ YMNSRG

हरौ श्रीयाद्दीव्यत्प्रवरललितंवल्लवीनां May this delightful sport of the mikmaids prevail with Hari.

8. अचलधृति

UUU UUU UUU UUU UUU U 16 breves 5NL

अचलधृतिरुदयतुसुकृतिहृदिखलु May he who sustained the mountain only shine into my virtuous heart.

9. गरुडरुत UUU U¯U ¯UU U¯U ¯U¯ ¯ NJBJRG

गरुडरुतं सुरारिभुजगेन्द्र संत्रासने It is like the cry of the eagle when it frightens the monstrous serpents of the giants.

XVII.

1. शिखरिणी

∪¯¯ ¯¯¯ | ∪∪∪ ∪∪¯ ¯∪∪ ∪¯ YMNSBLG

करादस्य भ्रष्टे ननु शिखरिणी ह्यस्य शिशो
विलीनाःस्मः सत्यं नियत मवधेयं तदखिलैः

See! should this mountain fall from the hand of this child, we shall certainly be destroyed: this should be thought of by us all.

2. पृथ्वीभर

∪¯∪ ∪∪¯ ∪¯ | ∪ ∪∪¯ ∪¯¯ ∪¯ JSJSYLG

दुरन्तदनुजेश्वरप्रकरदुःखपृथ्वीभरं The misery of the earth corrupted by the wicked giants.

3. वंशपत्रपतित

¯∪∪ ¯∪¯ ∪∪∪ ¯ ‖ ∪∪ ∪∪∪ ∪¯ BRNBNLG

नूतनवंशपत्रपतितं रजनि जललवं A drop of water fallen by night upon a fresh leaf.

4. मन्दाक्रान्ता

¯¯¯ ¯ | ∪∪ ∪∪∪ ¯ ‖ ¯∪¯ ¯∪¯ ¯ MBN2TGā

मन्दाक्रान्ता तदनुनियतं वश्यता मेति बाला By slow and persevering efforts the maid is subdued.

5. हरिणी

∪∪∪ ∪∪¯ ‖ ¯¯¯ ¯ ‖ ∪¯ ∪∪¯ ∪¯ NSMRSLG

व्यधित सविधि नेत्रे नीत्वा ध्रुवं हरिणी गणात् Bramha took the deer's eyes and gave them (to these women).

6. नर्दटक, or, with another cæsura, कोकिलक. This may have a pause at the 7th and 13th syllables.

∪∪∪ ∪¯∪ ¯∪∪ ∪¯∪ ∪¯∪ ∪¯ NJB2JLG

रुचिर पदावली घटितनर्दटकेनकविः The poet (describes) him in many pleasing verses of this kind.

7. हारिणी

––– – ‖ UU UUU ––– U ‖ –– U– MBNMYLG

सा कंसारे रमणि नकथं राधा मनोहारिणी How is it possible that Rādhā should not captivate Krishṇa's foe.

8. भाराक्रान्ता

––– – ‖ UU UUU – ‖ U– UU– U– MBNRSLG

भाराक्रान्ता ममतनुरियं गिरीन्द्र विधारणात् This body of mine is oppressed with sustaining the great mountain.

XVIII.

1. कुसमितलता

––– –– ‖ U UUU U– ‖ – U–– U–– MTN3Y

क्रीडाकालिन्दी ललित लहरी वारिभिर्दा क्षिणात्यै

र्वातैः खेलद्भिः कुसुमितलता वेल्लिता मन्दमन्दं

The flowering shrubs, slightly shaken by the southern breezes which raise a gentle swell in the playful Yamunā.

2. नन्दन

UUU U–U –UU U– ‖ U –U– –U– NJBJ2R

क्षितिजन नन्दनं व्रजसखे सुखाय वृन्दावनं O friend! go to the Vrinda wood, the delight of the earth, for happiness.

3. नाराच UUU UUU – ‖ U– –U– –U– –U– 2N4R

ननु विकिरति नेत्रनाराचमेषातिहृच्छेदनं Lo! she sends the heart-piercing arrow from her eye.

4. चित्रलेखा

––– – ‖ UU UUU U– ‖ – U–– U–– MBN3Y

प्रीतं तस्यां नयनयुगमभूत् चित्रलेखाद्भुतायां His dear eyes were fixed on this wondrous beautiful creature.

5. शार्दूल ललित

––– UU– U–U UU– ––U UU– MSJSYS

कृत्वा कंसमृगे पराक्रम विधिं शार्दूल ललितं Kamsa having by his power formed himself into a mimic tiger for hunting the deer.

XIX.

1. मेघविस्फूर्जिता

⏑-- --- ‖ ⏑⏑⏑ ⏑⏑- ‖ -⏑- -⏑- - YMNS2RG

निशानृत्य द्विद्युद्दि लसित लसन्मेघविस्फूर्जिताचेत् If the clouds at night are luminous with the vivid flashes of lightning.

2. छाया Like the preceding, only instead of -⏑- -⏑- it has ⏑-- ⏑--

नतस्त्वां ग्रेम्छायामुपगतवतां संसार तीव्रा तपः The distresses of life do not affect those who have taken refuge in the shadow of his feet.

3. शार्दूलविक्रीडित

--- ⏑⏑- ⏑-⏑ ⏑⏑- ‖ --⏑ --⏑ - MSJS2TG

नप्रेषे भवतां छते भवमहा शार्दूलविक्रीडितं I will not trouble you with this wide gaping tiger of a world.

4. सुरसा

--- -⏑- - ‖ ⏑⏑ ⏑⏑⏑ ⏑- ‖ - ⏑⏑⏑ - MRBNYNG

गोविन्दो वल्लवीनामधर रससुधं प्राप्य सुरसां Govinda obtained delicious nectar of the milkmaids.

5. फुल्लदाम

--- -- ‖ ⏑⏑⏑ ⏑⏑⏑ - ‖ -⏑ --⏑ -- MGā2N2TGā

माली दैत्तारे र्न्यपतदनु पमं स्वस्तरोः फुल्लदाम An unparalleled branch of flowers from the celestial tree fell on the head of the opposer of the demons.

XX.

1. सुवदना

--- -⏑- - ‖ ⏑⏑ ⏑⏑⏑ ⏑- ‖ - -⏑⏑ ⏑- MRBNYBLG

आनन्दाश्रु स्नुताक्षी ‖ वसति सुवदना ‖ योगी कर सिक्ता Filled with ecstasy she dwells, having her eyes full of tears of joy.

2. गीतिका

UU– U–U U–U –UU –U– UU– U– S2JBRSLG

विदधे हरिं खलुवल्लवी जनचारु चामर गीतिका (The flute) attended with the fanning and singing of the milkmaids, inspired Hari.

3. वृत्त

–U– ––U ॥ –U– ––U ॥ –U– ––U ॥ –U RTRTRTGL

चित्रवृत्तकी तथा निसर्गरम्यदेहरूपविभ्रमैश्च (He pleases) by the various movements and gestures of his enchanting form.

4. शोभा

U–– ––– UUU UUU ––U ––U –– YM2N2TGā

महाशोभा मौली मिलद्दलिपटलैः कृष्ण सा कापिवल्ली Krishṇa! there is a certain creeper having its head adorned with a multitude of bees.

XXI.

1. स्रग्धरा

––– –U– – ॥ UUU UUU – ॥ –U– –U– – MRG,NNG,RRG

मूर्त्तिर्गोपस्य विष्णो ॥ रवतुजगतिवः ॥ स्रग्धराहारहारा May the body of Vishṇu the herdsman, wearing a wreath and a necklace of pearls, preserve you in the world.

2. सरसी

UUU U–U –UU UUU UUU UUU –U– NJB3NR

व्यरचयदच्युतो व्रजमृगी नयनासरसीषु विभ्रमं The imperishable one was versed in amours with the deer-eyed stream-like maids of Vraja.

XXII.

1. हंसी

––– ––– –– ॥ UUU UUU UUU UUU –– 2MGā,4NGā

कंसराते पद्मस्वैषा ॥ सरभस मतिरिह विलसति हंसी See, Hari, how the agile swan is playing amid the lilies.

2. मदिरा

‾UU ‾UU ‾UU ‾UU ‖ ‾UU ‾UU ‾UU ‾ 7BG

माधवमासिविकस्वर केशर पुष्परसम्मदिरामुदिता: Tipsy with the pure juice of the opening flowers of spring.

XXIII.

1. अद्रितनया

UUU U‾U ‾U ‖ U U‾U ‾ ‖ UU U‾U UU‾ NJBJBJS

क्षितिवलये ऽखि। कंसभ्रमनखवेति तमवो ऽदद्रि तनया The daughter of the mountain said, etc.

2. मत्ताक्रीड

—— —— —— ‖ U UUU U ‖ UU UUU UUU UU‾ MMT4NS

मुग्धोमीलमत्ताक्रीडं मधु समय सुलभमधुरमधुरसात् Full of sport from the sweet honey, easily obtained in spring.

XXIV. तन्वी

‾UU ‾‾U U ‖ UU UU‾ ‖ ‾UU ‾UU UUU U‾‾

Each line may be divided thus, according to the cæsura pause. ‾UU ‾‾ UUUU UU‾ BGāNLS

Followed by ‾UU ‾UU UUUU ‾‾ 2BNLGā

माधव। मुग्धे। मधुकरविरुतै:
कोकिल। कूजित। मलयस। मीरै:
कम्पमु। पेता। मलयजसलिलै:
स्रावनतो ऽप्यविगततनुदाहा
पद्मपलाशै विरचितशयने
देहजसंज्वर भरपरिदूने
निश्वसतीसा मुकु रतिपक्षं
ध्यानलये तवनिवसति तन्वी

Thy fair one, o Mādhava, is dwelling in solitude, trembling at the mountain breezes, which are attended with the song of the cuckoo, and the hum of the wanton bees of spring; yet glowing with heat through having bathed in sandal water, and reclining on a bed composed of lotos leaves, which are greatly agitated by the heat arising from the body.

XXV. क्रौञ्चपदा, which like the preceding may be divided into two lines. Such metres might be considered not uniform but alternate.

‾UU ‾‾ ‾UU ‾‾ B Gā B Gā
UUUU UUUU UUUU UU‾ 3 N L S

क्रौञ्चप। दाली। चिह्नत तीरा
मदकल। खगकुल। कलकल। रुचिरा
फुल्लस। रोज। श्रेणि वि। लासा
मधुमु दि। तमधुप। रवरभ। सकरी
फेनविलास। प्रोज्ज्वल। हासा
ललित ल। हरि भर। पुलकित। सुतनुः
पश्य। हरे सौ। कस्य न। चेतो
हरति तरलगति। रिह मि। रजा

See, Hari! whose mind does not the swift Yamunā captivate? which has its sides impressed with the footsteps of paddy birds, is rendered vocal with the sweetest notes, adorned with full-blown lotoses, rendered enchanting by the hum of bees tipsy with honey, having its surface covered with bright foam, and beauteous with rolling waves.

XXVI. भुजङ्गविजृम्भित, thus divided at the pauses,

‾‾‾‾ ‾‾ ‾‾ 2 M Gā
UUUU UUUUU U‾ 3 N L G
U‾U U‾U ‾ 2 J G

वल्लभागस्त्रीभि र्भक्त्या
मुकुलित करकमलयुग

कृतस्तुतिरच्युतः
पायाद्व म्छिन्दग् कालिन्दी
ह्रदकृत निजवसति मृह
भुजङ्गविषृ म्भितं

May Achyuta preserve you, who is worshipped with uplifted hands by the affrighted female serpents, and who destroys the pride of the tremendous snake dwelling in a bed of the Yamunā.

XXVII. In this class are placed the Dandaka, already described; and other modes of composition for which there are no rules.

THE UDGATA OR ODES उद्गता

There are some wild carols seldom reducible to prosodial rules, wherein the poet follows his fancy, "numerisque fertur lege solutis," as Horace says. Mr. Colebrooke (p. 131) cites the following from the twelfth canto of the Kirāt Arjunīya: wherein, as in the fifteenth canto of Magha's epic poem, the Udgatā occurs.

UU¯ U¯U UUU ¯ NJNG
UUU UU¯ U¯U ¯ NSJG
¯UU UUU U¯U U¯ BNJLG
UU¯ U¯U UU¯ U¯U ¯ SJSJG

अथतत्रपाण्डु तनयेन
सदसि विहितं मधुद्विषः
मानम सहतनचेदिपतिः
परवृद्धि मत्सरिमनोहि मानिनां

But the king of the Chēdis was impatient of the honours which the son of Pāndu commanded to be shown in that assembly to the foe of Madhu; for the mind of the proud is envious of the prosperity of others.

Another variety, named ललित runs thus (G.D. Yates 444):

⏑⏑– ⏑–⏑ ⏑⏑– – SJSG
⏑⏑⏑ ⏑⏑– –⏑– – NSRG
⏑⏑⏑ ⏑⏑⏑ –⏑⏑ – 2NBG
⏑⏑– ⏑–⏑ ⏑⏑– ⏑–⏑ – SJSJG

विलसास गोपतरुणीषु
तरंगितनया प्रभोज्ज्वला
कृष्ण नयन चकोर युगे दधती
सुधांशु किरणो र्मिविभ्रमं

The resplendent Yamunā glides briskly among the youthful shepherdesses, reflecting the tremulous light of the moon's beams on the bright eyes of Krishṇa (Yates).

Another kind of Lalita.

⏑⏑– ⏑–⏑ ⏑⏑– – SJSG
⏑⏑⏑ ⏑⏑– ⏑– ⏑– NSJG
⏑⏑⏑ ⏑⏑⏑ ⏑⏑– ⏑⏑– 2N2S
⏑⏑– ⏑–⏑ ⏑⏑– ⏑–⏑ – SJSJG

व्रजसुन्दरी समुदयेन
मुदितमना सा प्रपीयते
हिमकर गलित मिवा मृतकं
ललितं मुरारि मुखचन्द्रविच्युतं

The sweet nectar distilled from the beaming face of Mura's enemy, is like that which falls from the moon, and is imbibed by the beauteous happy youth of Vraja.

Another variety of Udgatā runs thus.

⏑⏑– ⏑–⏑ ⏑⏑– ⏑ SJSG
⏑⏑⏑ ⏑⏑– ⏑–⏑ – NSJG
–⏑⏑ ⏑⏑⏑ ⏑–⏑⏑ – BNJLG
⏑⏑– ⏑–⏑ ⏑⏑– ⏑–⏑ – SJSJG

अथवासवस्यवचनेन

रुचिरवदनस्त्रिलोचनं

क्लान्तिरहितमभिराधयितुं

विधिवत्तपांसिविदधेधनंजयः

Then Dhananjaya (Vulcan) at the command of Indra with a pleasing countenance performed the appointed austerities to secure the favour of the tireless three-eyed one." (Id. p. 385.)

Another variety, called Saurabhaca (ib. p. 386).

∪∪– ∪–∪ ∪∪– ∪	SJSG
∪∪∪ ∪∪∪ –∪– ∪–	NNRLG
–∪– ∪∪∪ –∪∪ –	RNBG
∪∪– ∪–∪ ∪∪– ∪–∪ –	SJSJG

परिभूतफुल्लशतपत्र

वदनविसृतगन्धविभ्रमा

कस्यहृन्नहरतीहहरे

मुखपद्मसौरभकलातवाद्भुता

O Hari! whose heart does not the astonishing sweet fragrance of thy lotos-lips enchant? for it far excels the scent proceeding from hundreds of blooming lilies.

The eighth book of the Māgha closes with this verse, which the commentator calls वृत्तमुन्नेयं an unknown metre.

1	इतिधौतपुरंध्रि मत्सरान्	*a*	∪∪– ∪∪ – ∪–∪ –
2	सरसिमज्जनेन	*b*	∪∪∪ ∪–∪ –∪
	श्रियमाप्तवतोतिशायिनी	*c*	∪∪– ∪∪– ∪–∪ –
	ममलांगभासः	*d*	∪∪ –∪– ∪
3	अवलोक्यतदैव यादवा	*e*	∪∪– ∪∪ –∪– ∪–
4	नपरवारराशि	*f*	∪∪∪ –––
	शिशिरेतरोचिषा	*g*	∪∪– –∪–
	प्यपांततीषुमंक्षुमीषे	*h*	∪–∪ –∪– ∪––

All this is one stanza, in four lines of unequal length marked 1, 2, 3, 4.

The divisions here marked *a, c, e,* are alike: the other lines are irregular. This metre does not appear in any work on prosody.

In the musical compositions, such as the Gītā Govinda, the laws of harmony supersede those of prosody; this very name instead of – – ∪ is accented at pleasure Gŏvĭnda: and Krishna often becomes (∪ – an iambus) Krĭshnā. The well-known song, first printed by Sir William Jones in his Essay on the Musical Modes of the Hindus, beginning ललित लवङ्गलता परिशीलन को- मल मलय समीरे etc., sufficiently exemplifies this liberty.

ON THE SANSKRIT SYMBOLS USED FOR NUMERALS.

In Sanskrit chronology, arithmetic, and explanations of the Prosody, numerals are often expressed by symbols: in words on the plan of a Memoria Technica. The cypher is expressed by *sky*, *space*, or any synonyme of those words. Any phrase for the *moon*, the *earth*, or the *body*, stands for *one*. The unit is usually named first. A date occurs, stated thus, "Rĭtu, naga, vārdhi, himāmsu; signifying the *six* seasons, the *eight* mountains, the *four* seas, and the moon: beginning from the unit the import is 1, 4, 8, 6. Again: "Śara, bāhu, Rāma, vasudhā" represent, 5, 2, 3, 1; that is, the year of Sālivahāna 1325. In an edition of the Rāmāyan the date is stated "Nayana, dharādha 'rshi nalina-vairi sankhya, Sādhāraṇa-nama sambat-sara," that is, "in the year titled Sādhāraṇa, having the number *eyes, hills, sages, moon.*" This is 2771, and denotes SS. 1772, answering to A.D. 1850. Each sign of the zodiac being assigned a separate sun, any name of the sun denotes *twelve*. In one inscription "a pair of suns" denotes 1212. "Nētra, Sūrya, Chandra" (eyes, suns, moon) represent 2, 12, 1: that is, 1122, eleven hundred and twenty-two.

Occasionally numerals are mingled with symbols: thus: "*Nav*' āmbara, *dwi*, himāmsu." Nine, sky, *two*, moon, that is (9, 0, 2, 1) 1209.

In most of the Sanskrit treatises on prosody such enigmatic names are used: thus in the Śārdūla metre, the pauses fall on the syllables denoted by the number of "Mārtāṇḍas" (suns; viz. twelfth), and of the Munis (sages; viz. seven).* This method increases the difficulty, and is therefore popular. Having been much embarassed by these refinements, I think an explanation may be useful. The same system appears in volumes on Mathematicks and Astronomy. Thus in Dr. H. Kern's translations from A'ryá Bhatta,† a verse (in the A'ryá metre) is cited:—

गुरुभगणा राशिगुणा आश्वयुजाद्या गुरोरब्दाः ॥
गुरुभगणानां संख्या जिनयमवेदर्तुहव्यभुगतुल्या ॥

"The revolutions of Jupiter, multiplied by the number of the signs (12) are the years of Jupiter, called Aṣwayuja, etc.: his revolutions are equal to the number of the Jinas (24) a couple (2) the Vedas (4) the seasons (6) the fires (3). (i.e. 364, 224)."

The method of decyphering this, is explained in the following pages.

Besides the names given by Mr. Prinsep, a set of Jyautisha phrases (marked J.) will also be noticed.

Each name has several synonyma: thus for Sea we may use Ocean, Neptune, etc.

The 0, cipher, is called kha, ananta, ākāśam, ambara, vyoma, denoting space, sky, heaven, the endless (circle).

1. Any name of the moon, Adonis; as Chandra, Indu, etc. The earth, prithvi, bhū, ku. The body, tanu, etc. (J.) Vana. alone, solitary; rūpa, form, face.

2. Paksha, a wing; netra, eye; bāhu, arm; hasta, hand;

* See the Sruta Bodha, printed in the Journal Asiatique, Dec. 1854, by M. Ed. Lancereau, who has added a translation in French.

† In the Journal of the Royal Asiatic Society, vol. xx. of 1863, p. 378.

karna, ear. Yamam, a brace, couple, pair. Champa or champaca, "the gold flower: because there are two species." (See Prinsep's Journal, vol. iii. p. 210.)

3. Any name of Fire (vahni, agni, Krishānu, Vaisvānara), because in the Yajna sacrifice three fires were lighted. 'Netra,' the three eyes of Siva. 'Rāma,' there being three heroes of this name (Synonymes, Dāsarāthī, etc.). 'Guṅa,' quality, called Sattwa, rajas, tamō, guṅah. 'Loka,' or 'jagat,' worlds: heaven, earth, and hell. 'Tricam,' a trio. [Sahōdara, a brother. J.]

4. The Vedas. Jala-nidhi, or Ambu (waters), as there are four seas. Yuga (the four Ages), or Krita (the golden age), being the earliest. Koshthu (the corners; of a square). [Bandhu, J. a kinsman.]

5. Arrows, or Indriya, the senses: Cupid having five arrows, supposed to denote the five senses. Ratna (gems), Breaths (prāna) Sons (Suta, putra, etc.), Elements (Bhūt).

6. Limbs (anga), Tastes (rasa), Tunes (rāga), Seasons (ritu), as the year is divided into six seasons. The Sciences (Tarka, etc.), Ari: or Śatru, being the senses or passions described as the "six foes" of our happiness: being the sources of temptation.

7. Sages (a muni, a rishi, etc.), or Atri, who is the first of the seven. Musical notes (ut, re, mi, etc., called Swara). Mountains (adri, naga, etc.), as there are seven of note; or the name of any one of them, as Himāvat. Horses (because the Sun has seven to his car). Principles, elements (dhātu, etc.). [Wives, J. as Kalatram.] Mārutā (the seven winds), thus mārutā yōjanē, seven leagues off.

8. Vasu (a certain tribe of demi-gods). Elephants (Gaja,

Danti, etc.), the eight that stand under the eight points of the heavens. [Fortune, as mangala, bhūti, etc. J.]

9. Randhra, orifices (eyes, ears, nostrils, etc). Planets (graha, including the sun and moon).

10. Sides (Dik, disha, etc.), the eight points of the compass, with the zenith and nadir. Pancti: thus Rāvana was pancti-grīva, ten-necked: a party or society of ten. In J. the word Karma is in use.

11. Siva or Rudra: eleven demi-gods so called. [J. adds the word lābha.]

12. Sūrya: because each month has its own sun. Pushkara, a set of 12, as 12 years. Also the signs of the zodiac. See a Jyotish poem in the R.A.S. Journal, 1863, p. 378.

Mr. Prinsep has given a longer list: but I do not find that the additional names are in use; a few, however, are well known: thus—

24. The Jinas, a set of gods worshipped by the Jainas (see R.A.S.J. 1863, p. 378).

32. Danta, Teeth: the number of the human teeth.

The following dates, a few out of many instances, exemplify the method. The numerals are those of the era of Sālivāhana, which commenced in A.D. 79. The year A.D. 1800 is ss. 1722, A.D. 1860 is ss. 1782. The dates now to be quoted are engraven on marble.

ss.

235 is expressed Pancha, Tricam, lochana: that is, five and three and eyes.

888. Vasv' asht' āshta. (R.A.S.J. 1826, vol. xx. part 3, p. 372.) Here the first word is a symbol, the others are plain numerals.

1012. Ravi (12), Vyoma (a zero), Indu (the moon).

1021. Sasi (moon), pacshi (sides), kha (sky), aikē (one). Colebrooke's Essays, ii. 391.

1119. Randhra (nine), subhr āmsu (moon), rūpa (form), nakshatra nāyaka (moon).

In the Sruta bōdha, a Sanskrit treatise on Prosody, there is printed Vēdair A'ndhrair yatra, etc., and the French version says that this alludes to an "A'ndhra dynasty of nine princes in Magadha." This is an error. In the Chhandō manjari it is more correctly printed 'randhra:' thus, Vēdair *randhrair* atau, ya sa gā *Mattamayurah.*

1181. Chandra (one), Kari (elephants), Sasānkau (two moons).

1225. Bāń ācshi yugmam sasi. That is (five) arrows, two pairs (eyes), and moon. In the R.A.S.J. iv. 124, this is misinterpreted 1245.

1325. Sara, bāhu, rāma, vasudhā. But in another inscription Sara, bhuja, rāma, chandra. In another, Sara, danta, chandra. Here danta (teeth) denotes thirty-two.

1343. Sasi, vahni, vēda, hara drik, 'Moon, fires, vedas, and Siva's single eye. In this instance the unit is named not first but last.

1458. Vasu, bāńa, bhuvana gańitē sakē. This is quoted by Westergaard in the introduction to his Radices Sanscriticæ (Bonn, 1841), but by oversight he has omitted the first numeral: as here printed it is only 458.

1753. Krishānu, Bān, āswa, śaśānka śakē. This is the date (A.D. 1831) of the book 'Nīti Sankalanah,' printed at Calcutta in the Bengali character.

1764. Vēd ārtu, sapt, ēndum itē sakē. Date of an edition of the Kuvalayānandam printed at Punā. In this the numeral *seven* is used.

1772 (A.D. 1850). Nayana, dharādhara, Rishi, Nalina Vairi: i.e. eyes, hills, sages, moon. Date of an edition of the Rāmāyan printed at Madras.

NUMERICAL SYMBOLS

WHEREIN ENGLISH WORDS ARE USED.

This is an effort to adapt European words to the Hindoo method. The reckoning commences at the right hand. Thus 1862 would be 'nine, six, eight, one,' or 'Muse, Spring, Ei.'

0. the cipher, zero, is expressed Air, space, sky. Egg, oval, round, globe, orb. Also by Greek letters, α, β, γ, δ, as will be shown.

1. Aries, Ram, Moon.

2. Taurus, Bull.

The rest are represented by words chiefly of one syllable, having so many letters.

3. Cat, dog, owl, elk, fox, bat.

4. Ship, boat, brig, tree, wood.

5. Horse, steed, racer, prize.

6. Season, spring, summer, autumn, winter.

7. Rainbow; either syllable is enough: rain, or bow.

8. Strength, Vic[toria]: abbreviated Vic.

9. Crocodile, alligator, telescope, telegraph (the first syllable suffices). The nine 'Muses.'

10. Pho[tograph], Archimedes, Coromandel.

11. Electricity, Nightingale, the French Onze.

12. Jury, Douze. Thus 1262 is Bull, spring, douze, or Taurus, summer, bull, Aries.

13. Mediterranean, Treize, Tred[ecim]. Thus 1362 is Bull, spring, treize.

14. Trans[formation], Cons[tantinople]. Thus 1496 is Spring, muse, Trans. In the rest I omit the Ten, which is common to all.

15. Any word connected with *hand*, as finger. Thus 1500 is Beta hand, and 1558 is Vic. horse, hand. 1515 is hand hand.

16. Any word connected with a bee, which has six feet and a six-sided cell. Thus 1646 is Spring, boat, bee; or Season, ship, winter, moon.

17. Any word connected with a week, as Sunday. Thus 1769 is Muse, spring, week; or thus, Cro, summer, bow, ram.

18. Ei. Thus 1815 is Hand Ei. 1869 is Tel, Spring, Ei. 1800 is Beta Ei.

19 is Cro Ram.

23 is Sky, bull; or Globe, Taurus.

A figure that is repeated is expressed by Two or Pair. Thus 1855 is Two Lights and Ei. A figure thrice used is expressed Thrice or Trio. Thus 1777 is Two Bows and a Week. And 1666 would be Spring, summer, and bee. Sky, spring, Ei is 1860.

Many ciphers together, as 000, 0000, are represented by letters of the alphabet. Thus C or Co is three ciphers; E or Eo is five ciphers. 40,000,000 is written Go West. Here G, being the seventh letter, stands for seven ciphers. Fo Spring = 6,000,000.

Greek or Hebrew letters may be used. Thus (Zeta being the sixth letter) Zeta-Spring = 6,000,000. Or, if we use Hebrew letters, Vau-Winter.

Or, a Greek *word* beginning with the requisite letter. Thus

Thetis Socrates = 800,000,000. Thus for Δ, denoting four ciphers, we may use Delphin.

Verses framed on these methods will be more easy to recollect than those given in Grey's Memoria Technica.

The same method may be pursued in other languages, the Cipher, One, and Two, being disposed of as already stated.

In French, 3, Rat, âne. 4, Lion, Chat, Mari, Ours. 5, Loire, Femme, Aigle, Seine. 6, Cheval, Enfant, Pascal. 7, Ecureil, Cupidon, Boileau, Fenelon. 8, Elephant, Rousseau. 9, Corneille, Massillon, Empereur.

In Greek, 3, *φως, θηρ, εαρ* (or, *ἁι χαριτες*). 4, *ερως, λεων, κυων*. 5, *Αθηνη, Ἑκτωρ*. 6, *Ὁμηρος, αρκτος*. 7, *Αλέκτωρ, χελιδων*. 8, *Σωκρατης φασιανος*. 9, *χαριτες, ἁι μουσαι.*

In Latin, 3, Ver, Lux, Pax. 4, Cura, Fors. 5, Domus, arbor. 6, Ensis, scutum. 7, Ovidius, Oceanus. 8, Victoria, certamen. 9, Virgilius, or Musæ.

THE END.

LINGUISTIC PUBLICATIONS

OF

TRÜBNER & CO.,

60, PATERNOSTER ROW, LONDON, E.C.

Ahlwardt.—COLLECTION OF ANCIENT ARABIAN POETS; Published with Critical and Bibliographical Notes, and with an Index of Variations in the Text, etc. By W. AHLWARDT, Professor of Oriental Languages at the University of Greifswald. Crown 8vo. cloth. (*In the press.*)

Alcock.—A PRACTICAL GRAMMAR of the JAPANESE LANGUAGE. By Sir RUTHERFORD ALCOCK, Resident British Minister at Jeddo. 4to. pp. 61, sewed. 18*s*.

Alcock.—FAMILIAR DIALOGUES in JAPANESE, with English and French Translations, for the use of Students. By Sir RUTHERFORD ALCOCK. 8vo. pp. viii. and 40, sewed. Paris and London, 1863. 5*s*.

Alger.—THE POETRY OF THE ORIENT. By WILLIAM ROUNSEVILLE ALGER, 8vo. cloth, pp. xii. and 337. 9*s*.

Andrews.—A DICTIONARY OF THE HAWAIIAN LANGUAGE, to which is appended an English-Hawaiian Vocabulary, and a Chronological Table of Remarkable Events. By LORRIN ANDREWS. 8vo. pp. 560, cloth. £1 11*s*. 6*d*.

Asher.—ON THE STUDY OF MODERN LANGUAGES IN GENERAL, and of the English Language in particular. An Essay. By DAVID ASHER, Ph.D. 12mo. pp. viii. and 80, cloth. 2*s*.

Asiatic Society.—JOURNAL OF THE ROYAL ASIATIC SOCIETY OF GREAT BRITAIN AND IRELAND, from the Commencement to 1863. First Series, complete in 20 Vols. 8vo., with many Plates. Price £10; or, in Single Numbers, as follows:—Nos. 1 to 14, 6*s*. each; No. 15, 2 Parts, 4*s*. each; No. 16, 2 Parts, 4*s*. each; No. 17, 2 Parts, 4*s*. each; No. 18, 6*s*. These 18 Numbers form Vols. I. to IX.—Vol. X., Part 1, op.; Part 2, 5*s*.; Part 3, 5*s*.—Vol. XI., Part 1, 6*s*.; Part 2 not published.—Vol. XII., 2 Parts, 6*s*. each.—Vol. XIII., 2 Parts, 6*s*. each.—Vol. XIV., Part 1, 5*s*.; Part 2 not published.—Vol. XV., Part 1, 6*s*.; Part 2, with Maps, 10*s*.—Vol. XVI., 2 Parts, 6*s*. each.—Vol. XVII., 2 Parts, 6*s*. each.—Vol. XVIII., 2 Parts, 6*s*. each.—Vol. XIX., Parts 1 to 4, 16*s*.—Vol. XX., 3 Parts, 4*s*. each.

Asiatic Society.—JOURNAL OF THE ROYAL ASIATIC SOCIETY OF GREAT BRITAIN AND IRELAND. *New Series.* Vol. I. In Two Parts. pp. iv. and 490. Price 16*s*.

CONTENTS.—I. Vajra-chhedika, the "Kin Kong King," or Diamond Sútra. Translated from the Chinese by the Rev. S. Beal, Chaplain, R.N.—II. The Páramitá-hridaya Sútra, or, in Chinese, "Mo-ho-pô-ye-po-lo-mih-to-sin-king," i.e. "The Great Páramitá Heart Sútra." Translated from the Chinese by the Rev. S. Beal, Chaplain, R.N.—III. On the Preservation of National Literature in the East. By Colonel F. J. Goldsmid.—IV. On the Agricultural, Commercial, Financial, and Military Statistics of Ceylon. By E. R. Power, Esq.—V. Contributions to a Knowledge of the Vedic Theogony and Mythology. By J. Muir, D.C.L., LL.D.—VI. A Tabular List of Original Works and Translations, published by the late Dutch Government of Ceylon at their Printing Press at Colombo. Compiled by Mr. Mat. P. J. Ondaatje, of Colombo.—VII. Assyrian and Hebrew Chronology compared, with a view of showing the extent to which the Hebrew Chronology of Ussher must be modified, in conformity with the Assyrian Canon. By J. W. Bosanquet, Esq.—VIII. On the existing Dictionaries of the Malay Language. By Dr. H. N. van der Tuuk.—IX. Bilingual Readings: Cuneiform and Phœnician. Notes on some Tablets in the British Museum, containing Bilingual Legends (Assyrian and Phœnician). By Major-General Sir H. Rawlinson, K.C.B., Director R.A.S.—X. Translations of Three Copper-plate Inscriptions of the Fourth Century A.D., and Notices of the Châlukya and Gurjjara Dynasties. By Professor J. Dowson, Staff College, Sandhurst.—XI. Yama and the Doctrine of a Future Life, according to the Rig-Yajur-, and Atharva-Vedas. By J. Muir, Esq., D.C.L., LL.D.—XII. On the Jyotisha Observation of the Place of the Colures, and the Date derivable from it. By William D. Whitney, Esq., Professor of Sanskrit in Yale College, New Haven, U.S.—Note on the preceding Article. By Sir Edward Colebrooke, Bart., M.P., President R.A.S.—XIII. Progress of the Vedic Religion towards Abstract Conceptions of the Deity. By J. Muir, Esq., D.C.L., LL.D.—XIV. Brief Notes on the Age and Authenticity of the Work of Aryabhata, Varâhamihira, Brahmagupta, Bhattotpala, and Bhâskarâchârya. By Dr. Bhâu Dâjî, Honorary Member R.A.S.—XV. Outlines of a Grammar of the Malagasy Language. By H. N. Van der Tuuk.—XVI. On the Identity of Xandrames and Krananda. By Edward Thomas, Esq.

Vol. II. In Two Parts. pp. 522. Price, 16*s*.

CONTENTS.—I. Contributions to a Knowledge of Vedic Theogony and Mythology. No. 2. By J. Muir, Esq.—II. Miscellaneous Hymns from the Rig- and Atharva-Vedas. By J. Muir,

Esq.—III. Five hundred questions on the Social Condition of the Natives of Bengal. By the Rev. J. Long.—IV. Short account of the Malay Manuscripts belonging to the Royal Asiatic Society. By Dr. H. N. van der Tuuk.—V. Translation of the Amitâbha Sûtra from the Chinese. By the Rev. S. Beal, Chaplain Royal Navy.—VI. The initial coinage of Bengal. By Edward Thomas, Esq.—VII. Specimens of an Assyrian Dictionary. By Edwin Norris, Esq.—VIII. On the Relations of the Priests to the other classes of Indian Society in the Vedic age By J. Muir, Esq.—IX. On the Interpretation of the Veda. By the same.—X. An attempt to Translate from the Chinese a work known as the Confessional Services of the great compassionate Kwan Yin, possessing 1000 hands and 1000 eyes. By the Rev. S. Beal, Chaplain Royal Navy. —XI. The Hymns of the Gaupâyanas and the Legend of King Asamâti. By Professor Max Müller, M.A., Honorary Member Royal Asiatic Society.—XII. Specimen Chapters of an Assyrian Grammar. By the Rev. E. Hincks, D.D., Honorary Member Royal Asiatic Society.

Vol. III. In Two Parts. pp. 516. With Photograph. 22*s.*

CONTENTS.—I. Contributions towards a Glossary of the Assyrian Language. By H. F. Talbot. —II. Remarks on the Indo-Chinese Alphabets. By Dr. A. Bastian.—III. The poetry of Mohamed Rabadan, Arragonese. By the Hon. H. E. J. Stanley.—IV. Catalogue of the Oriental Manuscripts in the Library of King's College, Cambridge. By Edward Henry Palmer, B.A., Scholar of St. John's College, Cambridge; Member of the Royal Asiatic Society; Membre de la Société Asiatique de Paris.—V. Description of the Amravati Tope in Guntur. By J. Fergusson, Esq., F.R.S.—VI. Remarks on Prof. Brockhaus' edition of the Kathâsarit-sâgara, Lambaka IX. XVIII. By Dr. H. Kern, Professor of Sanskrit in the University of Leyden.—VII. The source of Colebrooke's Essay "On the Duties of a Faithful Hindu Widow." By Fitzedward Hall, Esq., M.A., D.C.L. Oxon. Supplement: Further detail of proofs that Colebrooke's Essay, "On the Duties of a Faithful Hindu Widow," was not indebted to the Vivâdabhangârnava. By Fitzedward Hall, Esq.—VIII. The Sixth Hymn of the First Book of the Rig Veda. By Professor Max Müller, M.A., Hon. M.R.A.S.—IX. Sassanian Inscriptions. By E. Thomas, Esq.—X. Account of an Embassy from Morocco to Spain in 1690 and 1691. By the Hon. H. E. J. Stanley.—XI. The Poetry of Mohamed Rabadan, of Arragon. By the Hon. H. E. J. Stanley.—XII. Materials for the History of India for the Six Hundred Years of Mohammadan rule, previous to the Foundation of the British Indian Empire. By Major W. Nassau Lees, LL.D., Ph.D.—XIII. A Few Words concerning the Hill people inhabiting the Forests of the Cochin State. By Captain G. E. Fryer, Madras Staff Corps, M.R.A.S.—XIV. Notes on the Bhojpurí Dialect of Hindí, spoken in Western Behar. By John Beames, Esq., B.C.S., Magistrate of Chumparun.

Asiatic Society.—TRANSACTIONS OF THE ROYAL ASIATIC SOCIETY OF GREAT BRITAIN AND IRELAND. Complete in 3 vols. 4to., 80 Plates of Fac similes, etc., cloth. London, 1827 to 1835. Published at £9 5*s.*; reduced to £1 11*s.* 6*d.*

The above contains contributions by Professor Wilson, G. C. Haughton, Davis, Morrison, Colebrooke, Humboldt, Dorn, Grotefend, and other eminent Oriental scholars.

Auctores Sanscriti. Edited for the Sanskrit Text Society, under the supervision of THEODOR GOLDSTÜCKER. Vol. I., containing the Jaiminîya-Nyâya-Mâlâ-Vistara. Parts I. to V., pp. 1 to 400, large 4to. sewed. 10*s.* each part.

Ballantyne.—ELEMENTS OF HINDÍ AND BRAJ BHÁKÁ GRAMMAR. By the late JAMES R. BALLANTYNE, LL.D. Second edition, revised and corrected Crown 8vo., pp. 44, cloth. 5*s.*

Ballantyne.—FIRST LESSONS IN SANSKRIT GRAMMAR; together with an Introduction to the Hitopadésa. Second edition. By JAMES R. BALLANTYNE, LL.D., Librarian of the India Office. 8vo. pp. viii. and 110, cloth. 1869. 5*s.*

Bartlett.—DICTIONARY OF AMERICANISMS: a Glossary of Words and Phrases colloquially used in the United States. By JOHN R. BARTLETT. Second Edition, considerably enlarged and improved. 1 vol. 8vo., pp. xxxii. and 524, cloth. 16*s.*

Beal.—TRAVELS OF FAH HIAN AND SUNG-YUN, Buddhist Pilgrims from China to India (400 A.D. and 518 A.D.) Translated from the Chinese, by S. BEAL (B.A. Trinity College, Cambridge), a Chaplain in Her Majesty's Fleet, a Member of the Royal Asiatic Society, and Author of a Translation of the Pratimôksha and the Amithâba Sûtra from the Chinese. Crown 8vo. pp. lxxiii. and 210, cloth, ornamental. 10*s.* 6*d.*

Beames.—OUTLINES OF INDIAN PHILOLOGY. With a Map, showing the Distribution of the Indian Languages. By JOHN BEAMES. Second enlarged and revised edition. Crown 8vo. cloth, pp. viii. and 96. 5*s.*

Bell.—ENGLISH VISIBLE SPEECH FOR THE MILLION, for communicating the Exact Pronunciation of the Language to Native or Foreign Learners, and for Teaching Children and illiterate Adults to Read in few Days. By ALEXANDER MELVILLE BELL, F.E.I.S., F.R.S.S.A., Lecturer on Elocution in University College, London. 4to. sewed, pp. 16. 1*s.*

Bell.—VISIBLE SPEECH; the Science of Universal Alphabetics, or Self-Interpreting Physiological Letters, for the Writing of all Languages in one Alphabet. Illustrated by Tables, Diagrams, and Examples. By ALEXANDER MELVILLE BELL, F.E.I.S., F.R.S.A., Professor of Vocal Physiology, etc. 4to., pp. 156, cloth. 15*s.*

Bellew.—A DICTIONARY OF THE PUKKHTO, OR PUKSHTO LANGUAGE, on a new and Improved System. With a reversed Part, or English and Pukkhto. By H. W. BELLEW, Assistant Surgeon, Bengal Army. Super Royal 8vo., pp. xii. and 356, cloth. 42*s.*

Bellew.—A GRAMMAR OF THE PUKKHTO OR PUKSHTO LANGUAGE, on a New and Improved System. Combining Brevity with Utility, and Illustrated by Exercises and Dialogues. By H. W. BELLEW, Assistant Surgeon, Bengal Army. Super-royal 8vo., pp. xii. and 156, cloth. 21*s.*

Bellows.—ENGLISH OUTLINE VOCABULARY for the use of Students of the Chinese, Japanese, and other Languages. Arranged by JOHN BELLOWS. With Notes on the writing of Chinese with Roman Letters. By Professor SUMMERS, King's College, London. 1 vol. crown 8vo., pp. 6 and 368, cloth. 6*s.*

Bellows.—OUTLINE DICTIONARY FOR THE USE OF MISSIONARIES, Explorers, and Students of Language. By MAX MÜLLER, M.A., Taylorian Professor in the University of Oxford. With an Introduction on the proper use of the ordinary English Alphabet in transcribing Foreign Languages. The Vocabulary compiled by JOHN BELLOWS. Crown 8vo. Limp morocco, pp. xxxi. and 368. 7*s.* 6*d.*

Benfey.—A PRACTICAL GRAMMAR OF THE SANSKRIT LANGUAGE, for the use of Early Students. By THEODOR BENFEY, Professor of Sanskrit in the University of Göttingen. Second, revised and enlarged, edition. Royal 8vo. pp. viii. and 296, cloth. 10*s.* 6*d.*

Beurmann.—VOCABULARY OF THE TIGRÉ LANGUAGE. Written down by MORITZ VON BEURMANN. Published with a Grammatical Sketch. By Dr. A. MERX, of the University of Jena. pp. viii. and 78, cloth. 3*s.* 6*d.*

Bholanauth Chunder.—THE TRAVELS OF A HINDOO TO VARIOUS PARTS OF BENGAL and Upper India. By BHOLANAUTH CHUNDER, Member of the Asiatic Society of Bengal. With an Introduction by J. Talboys Wheeler, Esq., Author of "The History of India." Dedicated, by permission, to His Excellency Sir John Laird Mair Lawrence, G.C.B., G.C.S.I., Viceroy and Governor-General of India, etc. In 2 volumes, crown 8vo., cloth, pp. xxv. and 440, viii. and 410. 21*s.*

Bigandet.—THE LIFE OR LEGEND OF GAUDAMA, the Budha of the Burmese, with Annotations. The ways to Neibban, and Notice on the Phongyies, or Burmese Monks. By the Right Reverend P. BIGANDET, Bishop of Ramatha, Vicar Apostolic of Ava and Pegu. 8vo. sewed, pp. xi., 538, and v. 18*s.*

Bleek.—A COMPARATIVE GRAMMAR OF SOUTH AFRICAN LANGUAGES. By Dr. W. H. I. BLEEK. Will be completed in Four Parts. Part I., pp. 104, sewed. 5*s.*

Bleek.—REYNARD IN SOUTH AFRICA; or, Hottentot Fables. Translated from the Original Manuscript in Sir George Grey's Library. By Dr. W. H. I. BLEEK, Librarian to the Grey Library, Cape Town, Cape of Good Hope. In one volume, small 8vo., pp. xxxi. and 94, cloth. 3*s.* 6*d.*

Bombay Sanskrit Series. Edited under the superintendence of G. BÜHLER, Ph. D., Professor of Oriental Languages, Elphinstone College, and F. KIELHORN, Ph. D., Superintendent of Sanskṛit Studies, Deccan College.

Already published.

1. PANCHATANTRA IV. AND V. Edited with Notes, by G. BÜHLER, Ph. D. Pp. 84, 16. 4*s.* 6*d.*
2. NÁGOJÍBHAṬṬA'S PARIBHÁSHENDUŚEKHARA. Edited and explained by F. KIELHORN, Ph. D. Part I., the Sanskṛit Text and various readings. pp. 116. 8*s.* 6*d.*
3. PANCHATANTRA II. AND III. Edited with Notes by G. BÜHLER, Ph. D. Pp. 86, 14, 2. 5*s.* 6*d.*
4. PANCHATANTRA I. Edited with Notes by F. KIELHORN, Ph.D. Pp. 114, 53. 8*s.* 6*d.*

Boyce.—A Grammar of the Kaffir Language.—By William B. Boyes, Wesleyan Missionary. Third Edition, augmented and improved, with Exercises, by William J. Davis, Wesleyan Missionary. 12mo. pp. xii. and 164, cloth, 8*s.*

Bowditch.—Suffolk Surnames. By N. I. Bowditch. Third Edition, 8vo. pp. xxvi. and 758, cloth. 7*s.* 6*d.*

Brice.—A Romanized Hindustani and English Dictionary. Designed for the use of Schools and for Vernacular Students of the Language. Compiled by Nathaniel Brice. New Edition, Revised and Enlarged. Post 8vo. cloth, pp. vi. and 357. Price 8*s.*

Brinton.—The Myths of the New World. A Treatise on the Symbolism and Mythology of the Red Races of America. By Daniel G. Brinton, A.M., M.D. Crown 8vo. cloth, pp. viii. and 308. 10*s.* 6*d.*

Brown.—The Dervishes; or, Oriental Spiritualism. By John P. Brown, Secretary and Dragoman of the Legation of the United States of America at Constantinople. With twenty-four Illustrations. 8vo. cloth, pp. viii. and 415. 14*s.*

Brown.—Carnatic Chronology. The Hindu and Mahomedan Methods of Reckoning Time explained: with Essays on the Systems; Symbols used for Numerals, a new Titular Method of Memory, Historical Records, and other subjects. By Charles Philip Brown, Member of the Royal Asiatic Society; late of the Madras Civil Service; Telugu Translator to Government; Senior Member of the College Board, etc.; Author of the Telugu Dictionaries and Grammar, etc. 4to. sewed, pp. xii. and 90. 10*s.* 6*d.*

Brown.—Sanskrit Prosody Explained. By Charles Philip Brown, Author of the Telugu Dictionary. In 1 vol. 8vo. cloth. [*In the press.*

Buddhaghosha.—Buddhaghosha's Parables: translated from Burmese by Captain H. T. Rogers, R.E. With an Introduction containing Buddha's Dhammapadam, or, Path of Virtue; translated from Pali by F. Max Müller. [*In the press.*

Burgess.—Surya-Siddhanta (Translation of the): A Text-book of Hindu Astronomy, with Notes and an Appendix, containing additional Notes and Tables, Calculations of Eclipses, a Stellar Map, and Indexes. By Rev. Ebenezer Burgess, formerly Missionary of the American Board of Commissioners of Foreign Missions in India; assisted by the Committee of Publication of the American Oriental Society. 8vo. pp. iv. and 354, boards. 15*s.*

Callaway.—Izinganekwane, Nensumansumane, Nezindaba, Zabantu (Nursery Tales, Traditions, and Histories of the Zulus). In their own words, with a Translation into English, and Notes. By the Rev. Henry Callaway, M.D. Volume I., 8vo. pp. xiv. and 378, cloth. Natal, 1866 and 1867. 16*s.*

Callaway.—The Religious System of the Amazulu. Part I. Unkulunkulu, or, the Tradition of Creation as existing among the Amazulu and other Tribes of South Africa, in their own words, with a translation into English, and Notes. By the Rev. Canon Callaway, M.D., 8vo. pp. 126, sewed. 1868.

Canones Lexicographici; or, Rules to be observed in Editing the New English Dictionary of the Philological Society, prepared by a Committee of the Society. 8vo., pp. 12, sewed. 6*d.*

Carpenter.—The Last Days in England of the Rajah Rammohun Roy. By Mary Carpenter, of Bristol. With Five Illustrations. 8vo. pp. 272, cloth. 7*s.* 6*d.*

Carr.—ఆంధ్రలోకోక్తిచంద్రిక. A Collection of Telugu Proverbs, Translated, Illustrated, and Explained; together with some Sanscrit Proverbs printed in the Devnâgarî and Telugu Characters. By Captain M. W. Carr, Madras Staff Corps. One Vol. and Supplement, royal 8vo. pp. 488 and 148. 24*s.*

Catlin.—O-Kee-Pa. A Religious Ceremony of the Mandans. By George Catlin. With 13 Coloured Illustrations. 4to. pp. 60, bound in cloth, gilt edges. 14*s.*

Chalmers.—The Origin of the Chinese; an Attempt to Trace the connection of the Chinese with Western Nations in their Religion, Superstitions, Arts, Language, and Traditions. By John Chalmers, A.M. Foolscap 8vo. cloth, pp. 78. 2*s.* 6*d.*

Chalmers.—The Speculations on Metaphysics, Polity, and Morality of "The Old Philosopher" Lau Tsze. Translated from the Chinese, with an Introduction by John Chalmers, M.A. Fcap. 8vo. cloth, xx. and 62. 4*s.* 6*d.*

Charnock.—Ludus Patronymicus; or, the Etymology of Curious Surnames. By Richard Stephen Charnock, Ph.D., F.S.A., F.R.G.S. In 1 vol. crown 8vo., pp. 182, cloth. 7*s.* 6*d.*

Charnock.—Verba Nominalia; or Words derived from Proper Names. By Richard Stephen Charnock, Ph. Dr. F.S.A., etc. 8vo. pp. 326, cloth. 14*s.*

Chaucer Society's Publications. *First Series.*

A Six-Text Print of Chaucer's Canterbury Tales, in parallel columns, from the following MSS.:—1. The Ellesmere. 2. The Hengwrt, 154. 3. The Cambridge Univ. Libr. Gg. 4, 27. 4. The Corpus Christi College, Oxford. 5. The Petworth. 6. The Lansdowne, 851.—Part I. The Prologue and Knight's Tale. (*Each of the above Texts are also published separately.*)

Second Series.

1. On Early English Pronunciation, with especial reference to Shakespeare and Chaucer, containing an investigation of the Correspondence of Writing with Speech in England, from the Anglo-Saxon period to the present day, preceded by a systematic notation of all spoken sounds, by means of the ordinary printing types. Including a re-arrangement of Prof. F. J. Child's Memoirs on the Language of Chaucer and Gower, and Reprints of the Rare Tracts by Salesbury on English, 1547, and Welch, 1567, and by Barcley on French, 1521. By Alexander J. Ellis, F.R.S., etc., etc. Part I. On the Pronunciation of the xivth, xvith, xviith, and xviiith centuries. 10*s.*
2. Essays on Chaucer; His Words and Works. Part I. 1. Ebert's Review of Sandras's *E'tude sur Chaucer, considére comme Imitateur des Trouvères*, translated by J. W. Van Rees Hoets, M.A., Trinity Hall, Cambridge, and revised by the Author.—II. A Thirteenth Century Latin Treatise on the *Chilindre*: "For by my *chilindre* it is prime of day" (*Shipmannes Tale*). Edited, with a Translation, by Mr. Edmund Brock, and illustrated by a Woodcut of the Instrument from the Ashmole MS., 1522.
3. A Temporary Preface to the Six-Text Edition of Chaucer's Canterbury Tales. Part I. Attempting to show the true order of the Tales, and the Days and Stages of the Pilgrimage, etc., etc. By F. J. Furnivall, Esq., M.A., Trinity Hall, Cambridge.

Chronique de Abou-Djafar-Mohammed-Ben-Djarir-Ben-Yezid Tabari. Traduite par Monsieur Hermann Zotenberg. Vol. I., 8vo. pp. 608, sewed. 7*s.* 6*d.* (*To be completed in Four Volumes.*)

Colenso.—First Steps in Zulu-Kafir: An Abridgement of the Elementary Grammar of the Zulu-Kafir Language. By the Right Rev. John W. Colenso, Bishop of Natal. 8vo. pp. 86, cloth. Ekukanyeni, 1859. 4*s.* 6*d.*

Colenso.—Zulu-English Dictionary. By the Right Rev. John W. Colenso, Bishop of Natal. 8vo. pp. viii. and 552, sewed. Pietermaritzburg, 1861. 15*s.*

Colenso.—First Zulu-Kafir Reading Book, two parts in one. By the Right Rev. John W. Colenso, Bishop of Natal. 16mo. pp. 44, sewed. Natal. 1*s.*

Colenso.—Second Zulu-Kafir Reading Book. By the same. 16mo. pp. 108, sewed. Natal. 3*s.*

Colenso.—Fourth Zulu-Kafir Reading Book. By the same. 8vo. pp. 160, cloth. Natal, 1859. 7*s.*

Colenso.—Three Native Accounts of the Visits of the Bishop of Natal in September and October, 1859, to Upmande, King of the Zulus; with Explanatory Notes and a Literal Translation, and a Glossary of all the Zulu Words employed in the same: designed for the use of Students of the Zulu Language. By the Right Rev. John W. Colenso, Bishop of Natal. 16mo. pp. 160, stiff cover. Natal, Maritzburg, 1860. 4*s.* 6*d.*

Coleridge.—A GLOSSARIAL INDEX to the Printed English Literature of the Thirteenth Century. By HERBERT COLERIDGE, Esq. 1 vol. 8vo. pp. 104, cloth. 2*s*. 6*d*.

Colleccao de Vocabulos e Frases usados na Provincia de S. Pedro, do Rio Grande do Sul, no Brasil. 12mo. pp. 32, sewed. 1*s*.

Contopoulos.—A LEXICON OF MODERN GREEK-ENGLISH AND ENGLISH MODERN GREEK. By N. CONTOPOULOS. First Part, Modern Greek-English. 8vo. cloth, pp. 460. 12*s*.

Dennys.—CHINA AND JAPAN. A complete Guide to the Open Ports of those countries, together with Pekin, Yeddo, Hong Kong, and Macao; forming a Guide Book and Vade Mecum for Travellers, Merchants, and Residents in general; with 56 Maps and Plans. By WM. FREDERICK MAYERS, F.R.G.S. H.M.'s Consular Service; N. B. DENNYS, late H.M.'s Consular Service; and CHARLES KING, Lieut. Royal Marine Artillery. Edited by N. B. DENNYS. In one volume. 8vo. pp. 600, cloth. £2 2*s*.

Döhne.—A ZULU-KAFIR DICTIONARY, etymologically explained, with copious Illustrations and examples, preceded by an introduction on the Zulu-Kafir Language. By the Rev. J. L. DÖHNE. Royal 8vo. pp. xlii. and 418, sewed. Cape Town, 1857. 21*s*.

Döhne.—THE FOUR GOSPELS IN ZULU. By the Rev. J. L. DÖHNE, Missionary to the American Board, C.F.M. 8vo. pp. 208, cloth. Pietermaritzburg, 1866. 5*s*.

Early English Text Society's Publications.

1. EARLY ENGLISH ALLITERATIVE POEMS. In the West-Midland Dialect of the Fourteenth Century. Edited by R. MORRIS, Esq., from an unique Cottonian MS. 16*s*.
2. ARTHUR (about 1440 A.D.). Edited by F. J. FURNIVALL, Esq., from the Marquis of Bath's unique M.S. 4*s*.
3. ANE COMPENDIOUS AND BREUE TRACTATE CONCERNYNG YE OFFICE AND DEWTIE OF KYNGIS, etc. By WILLIAM LAUDER. (1556 A.D.) Edited by F. HALL, Esq., D.C.L. 4*s*.
4. SIR GAWAYNE AND THE GREEN KNIGHT (about 1320-30 A.D.). Edited by R. MORRIS, Esq., from an unique Cottonian MS. 10*s*.
5. OF THE ORTHOGRAPHIE AND CONGRUITIE OF THE BRITAN TONGUE; a treates, noe shorter than necessarie, for the Schooles, be ALEXANDER HUME. Edited for the first time from the unique MS. in the British Museum (about 1617 A.D.), by HENRY B. WHEATLEY, Esq. 4*s*.
6. LANCELOT OF THE LAIK. Edited from the unique MS. in the Cambridge University Library (ab. 1500), by the Rev. WALTER W. SKEAT, M.A. 8*s*.
7. THE STORY OF GENESIS AND EXODUS, an Early English Song, of about 1250 A.D. Edited for the first time from the unique MS. in the Library of Corpus Christi College, Cambridge, by R. MORRIS, Esq. 8*s*.
8. MORTE ARTHURE; the Alliterative Version. Edited from ROBERT THORNTON'S unique MS. (about 1440 A.D.) at Lincoln, by the Rev. GEORGE PERRY, M.A., Prebendary of Lincoln. 7*s*.
9. ANIMADVERSIONS UPPON THE ANNOTACIONS AND CORRECTIONS OF SOME IMPERFECTIONS OF IMPRESSIONES OF CHAUCER'S WORKES, reprinted in 1598; by FRANCIS THYNNE. Edited from the unique MS. in the Bridgewater Library. By G. H. KINGSLEY, Esq., M.D. 4*s*.
10. MERLIN, OR THE EARLY HISTORY OF KING ARTHUR. Edited for the first time from the unique MS. in the Cambridge University Library (about 1450 A.D.), by HENRY B. WHEATLEY, Esq. Part I. 2*s*. 6*d*.
11. THE MONARCHE, and other Poems of Sir David Lyndesay. Edited from the first edition by JOHNE SKOTT, in 1552, by FITZEDWARD HALL, Esq., D.C.L. Part I. 3*s*.
12. THE WRIGHT'S CHASTE WIFE, a Merry Tale, by Adam of Cobsam (about 1462 A.D.), from the unique Lambeth MS. 306. Edited for the first time by F. J. FURNIVALL, Esq., M.A. 1*s*.

Early English Text Society's Publications—*continued.*

13. SEINTE MARHERETE, ÞE MEIDEN ANT MARTYR. Three Texts of ab. 1200, 1310, 1330 A.D. First edited in 1862, by the Rev. OSWALD COCKAYNE, M.A., and now re-issued. 2*s.*
14. KYNG HORN, with fragments of Floriz and Blaunchefiur, and the Assumption of the Blessed Virgin. Edited from the MS. in the Library of the University of Cambridge and the British Museum, by the Rev. J. RAWSON LUMBY. 3*s.* 6*d.*
15. POLITICAL, RELIGIOUS, AND LOVE POEMS, from the Lambeth MS., No. 306, and other sources. Edited by F. J. FURNIVALL, Esq., M.A. 7*s.* 6*d.*
16. A TRETICE IN ENGLISH breuely drawe out of þ book of Quintis essencijs in Latyn, þ Hermys þ prophete and king of Egipt after þ flood of Noe, fader of Philosophris, hadde by reuelaciouns of an aungil of God to him sente. Edited from the Sloane MS. 73, by F. J. FURNIVALL, Esq., M.A. 1*s.*
17. PARALLEL EXTRACTS from 29 Manuscripts of PIERS PLOWMAN, with Comments, and a Proposal for the Society's Three-text edition of this Poem. By the Rev. W. SKEAT, M.A. 1*s.*
18. HALI MEIDENHEAD, about 1200 A.D. Edited for the first time from the MS. (with a translation) by the Rev. OSWALD COCKAYNE, M.A. 1*s.*
19. THE MONARCHE, and other Poems of Sir David Lyndesay. Part II., the Complaynt of the King's Papingo, and other minor Poems. Edited from the First Edition by F. HALL, Esq., D.C L. 3*s.* 6*d.*
20. SOME TREATISES BY RICHARD ROLLE DE HAMPOLE. Edited from Robert of Thornton's MS. ab. 1440 A.D., by Rev. GEORGE G. PERRY, M.A. 1*s.*
21. MERLIN, OR THE EARLY HISTORY OF KING ARTHUR. Part II. Edited by HENRY B. WHEATLEY, Esq. 4*s.*
22. THE ROMANS OF PARTENAY, OR LUSIGNEN. Edited for the first time from the unique MS. in the Library of Trinity College, Cambridge, by the Rev. W. W. SKEAT. M.A. 6*s.*
23. DAN MICHEL'S AYENBITE OF INWYT, or Remorse of Conscience, in the Kentish dialect, 1340 A.D. Edited from the unique MS. in the British Museum, by RICHARD MORRIS, Esq. 10*s.* 6*d.*
24. HYMNS OF THE VIRGIN AND CHRIST; THE PARLIAMENT OF DEVILS, and Other Religious Poems. Edited from the Lambeth MS. 853, by F. J. FURNIVALL, M.A. 3*s.*
25. THE STACIONS OF ROME, and the Pilgrim's Sea-Voyage and Sea-Sickness, with Clene Maydenhod. Edited from the Vernon and Porkington MSS., etc., by F. J. FURNIVALL, Esq., M.A. 1*s.*
26. RELIGIOUS PIECES IN PROSE AND VERSE. Containing Dan Jon Gaytrigg's Sermon; The Abbaye of S. Spirit; Sayne Jon, and other pieces in the Northern Dialect. Edited from Robert of Thorntone's MS. (ab. 1460 A.D.) by the Rev. G. PERRY, M.A. 2*s.*
27. MANIPULUS VOCABULORUM: a Rhyming Dictionary of the English Language, by PETER LEVINS (1570). Edited, with an Alphabetical Index, by HENRY B. WHEATLEY. 12*s.*
28. THE VISION OF WILLIAM CONCERNING PIERS PLOWMAN, together with Vita de Dowel, Dobet et Dobest. 1362 A.D., by WILLIAM LANGLAND. The earliest or Vernon Text; Text A. Edited from the Vernon MS., with full Collations, by Rev. W. W. SKEAT, M.A. 7*s.*
29. OLD ENGLISH HOMILIES AND HOMILETIC TREATISES. (Sawles Warde, and the Wohunge of Ure Lauerd: Ureisuns of Ure Louerd and of Ure Lefdi, etc.) of the Twelfth and Thirteenth Centuries. Edited from MSS. in the British Museum, Lambeth, and Bodleian Libraries; with Introduction, Translation, and Notes. By RICHARD MORRIS. *First Series.* Part I. 7*s.*
30. PIERS, THE PLOUGHMAN'S CREDE (about 1394). Edited from the MSS. by the Rev. W. W. SKEAT, M.A. 2*s.*
31. INSTRUCTIONS FOR PARISH PRIESTS. By JOHN MYRC. Edited from Cotton M.S. Claudius A. II., by EDWARD PEACOCK, Esq., F.S.A., etc., etc. 4*s.*

Early English Text Society's Publications—*continued.*

32. THE BABEES BOOK, Aristotle's A B C, Urbanitatis, Stans Puer ad Mensam, The Lytille Childrenes Lytil Boke. THE BOKES OF NURTURE of Hugh Rhodes and John Russell, Wynkyn de Worde's Boke of Kervynge, The Booke of Demeanor, The Boke of Curtasye, Seager's Schoole of Vertue, etc., etc. With some French and Latin Poems on like subjects, and some Forewords on Education in Early England. Edited by F. J. FURNIVALL, M.A., Trin. Hall, Cambridge. 15*s.*

33. THE BOOK OF THE KNIGHT DE LA TOUR LANDRY, 1372. A Father's Book for his Daughters, Edited from the Harleian MS. 1764, by THOMAS WRIGHT, Esq., M.A., and Mr. WILLIAM ROSSITER. 8*s.*

34. OLD ENGLISH HOMILIES AND HOMILETIC TREATISES. (Sawles Warde, and the Wohunge of Ure Lauerd: Ureisuns of Ure Louerd and of Ure Lefdi, etc.) of the Twelfth and Thirteenth Centuries. Edited from MSS. in the British Museum, Lambeth, and Bodleian Librsries; with Introduction, Translation, and Notes, by RICHARD MORRIS. *First Series.* Part 2. 8*s.*

35. SIR DAVID LYNDESAY'S WORKS. PART 3. The Historie of ane Nobil and Wailzeand Sqvyer, WILLIAM MELDRUM, umqvhyle Laird of Cleische and Bynnis, compylit be Sir DAUID LYNDESAY of the Mont *alias* Lyoun King of Armes. With the Testament of the said Williame Meldrum, Squyer, compylit alswa be Sir Dauid Lyndesay, etc. Edited by F. HALL, D.C.L. 2*s.*

36. MERLIN, OR THE EARLY HISTORY OF KING ARTHUR. A Prose Romance (about 1450–1460 A.D.), edited from the unique MS. in the University Library, Cambridge, by HENRY B. WHEATLEY. With an Essay on Arthurian Localities, by J. S. STUART GLENNIE, Esq. Part III. 1869. 12*s.*

37. SIR DAVID LYNDESAY'S WORKS. Part IV. Ane Satyre of the thrie estaits, in commendation of vertew and vitvperation of vyce. Maid be Sir DAVID LINDESAY, of the Mont, *alias* Lyon King of Armes. At Edinbvrgh. Printed be Robert Charteris, 1602. Cvm privilégio regis. Edited by F. HALL, Esq., D.C.L. 4*s.*

Extra Series.

1. THE ROMANCE OF WILLIAM OF PALERNE (otherwise known as the Romance of William and the Werwolf). Translated from the French at the command of Sir Humphrey de Bohun, about A.D. 1350, to which is added a fragment of the Alliterative Romance of Alisaunder, translated from the Latin by the same author, about A.D. 1340; the former re-edited from the unique MS. in the Library of King's College, Cambridge, the latter now first edited from the unique MS. in the Bodleian Library, Oxford. By the Rev. WALTER W. SKEAT, M.A. 8vo. sewed, pp. xliv. and 328. £1 6*s.*

2*a.* ON EARLY ENGLISH PRONUNCIATION, with especial reference to Shakespeare and Chaucer; containing an investigation of the Correspondence of Writing with Speech in England, from the Anglo-Saxon period to the present day, preceded by a systematic Notation of all Spoken Sounds by means of the ordinary Printing Types; including a re-arrangement of Prof. F. J. Child's Memoirs on the Language of Chaucer and Gower, and reprints of the rare Tracts by Salesbury on English, 1547, and Welch, 1567, and by Barcley on French, 1521. By ALEXANDER J. ELLIS, F.R.S. Part I. On the Pronunciation of the XIVth, XVIth, XVIIth, and XVIIIth centuries. 8vo. sewed, pp. viii. and 416. 10*s.*

3. CAXTON'S BOOK OF CURTESYE, printed at Westminster about 1477–8, A.D., and now reprinted, with two MS. copies of the same treatise, from the Oriel MS. 79, and the Balliol MS. 354. Edited by FREDERICK J. FURNIVALL, M.A. 8vo. sewed, pp. xii. and 58. 5*s.*

4. THE LAY OF HAVELOK THE DANE; composed in the reign of Edward I., about A.D. 1280. Formerly edited by Sir F. MADDEN for the Roxburghe Club, and now re-edited from the unique MS. Laud Misc. 108, in the Bodleian Library, Oxford, by the Rev. WALTER W. SKEAT, M.A. 8vo. sewed, pp. lv. and 160. 10*s.*

Early English English Text Society's Publications—*continued.*

5. Chaucer's Boetius. [*In the press.*
6. The Romance of the Chenelere Assigne. Re-edited from the unique manuscript in the British Museum, with a Preface, Notes, and Glossarial Index, by Henry H. Gibbs, Esq., M.A. 8vo. sewed, pp. xviii. and 38. 3*s.*

Edda Saemundar Hinns Froda—The Edda of Saemund the Learned. From the Old Norse or Icelandic. Part I. with a Mythological Index. 12mo. pp. 152, cloth, 3*s.* 6*d.* Part II. with Index of Persons and Places. By Benjamin Thorpe. 12mo. pp. viii. and 172, cloth. 1866. 4*s.*; or in 1 Vol. complete, 7*s.* 6*d.*

Eger and Grime; an Early English Romance. Edited from Bishop Percy's Folio Manuscript, about 1650 A.D. By John W. Hales, M.A., Fellow and late Assistant Tutor of Christ's College, Cambridge, and Frederick J. Furnivall, M.A., of Trinity Hall, Cambridge. 1 vol. 4to. (only 100 copies printed), bound in the Roxburgh style. pp. 64. Price 10*s.* 6*d.*

Elliot.—The History of India, as told by its own Historians. The Muhammadan Period. Edited from the Posthumous Papers of the late Sir H. M. Elliot, K.C.B., East India Company's Bengal Civil Service, by Prof. John Dowson, M.R.A.S., Staff College, Sandhurst. Vols. I. and II. With a Portrait of Sir H. M. Elliot. 8vo. pp xxxii. and 542, x. and 580, cloth. 18*s.* each.

Elliot.—Memoirs on the History, Philology, and Ethnic Distribution of the Races of the North-west Provinces of India; being an amplified Edition of the Glossary of Indian Terms. By the late Sir H. M. Elliot, K.C.B. Arranged from MS. materials collected by him, and Edited by John Beames, Esq., M.R.A.S., Bengal Civil Service, Member of the Asiatic Society of Bengal, The Philological Society of London, and the Société Asiatique of Paris. In two volumes. 8vo. [*In the press.*

Ethnological Society of London (The Journal of the). Edited by Professor Huxley, F.R.S., President of the Society; George Busk, Esq., F.R.S.; Sir John Lubbock, Bart., F.R.S.; Colonel A. Lane Fox, Hon. Sec.; Thomas Wright, Esq., Hon. Sec.; Hyde Clarke, Esq.; Sub-Editor; and Assistant Secretary, J. H. Lamprey, Esq. Published Quarterly. 8vo. pp. 88, sewed, 8*s.*

Contents of the April Number, 1869.—Flint Instruments from Oxfordshire and the Isle of Thanet. (Illustrated.) By Colonel A. Lane Fox.—The Westerly Drifting of Nomads. By H. H. Howorth.—On the Lion Shilling. By Hyde Clarke.—Letter on a Marble Armlet. By H. W. Edwards.—On a Bronze Spear from Lough Gur, Limerick. (Illustrated.) By Col. A. Lane Fox.—On Chinese Charms. By W. H. Black.—Proto-ethnic Condition of Asia Minor. By Hyde Clarke.—On Stone Implements from the Cape. (Illustrated.) By Sir J. Lubbock.—Cromlechs and Megalithic Structures. By H. M. Westropp.—Remarks on Mr. Westropp's Paper. By Colonel A. Lane Fox.—Stone Implements from San José. By A. Steffens.—On Child-bearing in Australia and New Zealand. By J. Hooker, M.D.—On a Pseudo-cromlech on Mount Alexander, Australia. By Acheson.—The Cave Cannibals of South Africa. By Layland.—Reviews: Wallace's Malay Archipelago (with illustrations); Fryer's Hill Tribes of India (with an illustration); Reliquiæ Aquitanicæ, etc.—Method of Photographic Measurement of the Human Frame (with an illustration). By J. H. Lamprey.—Notes and Queries.

Facsimiles of Two Papyri found in a Tomb at Thebes. With a a Translation by Samuel Birch, LL.D., F.S.A., Corresponding Member of the Institute of France, Academies of Berlin, Herculaneum, etc., and an Account of their Discovery. By A. Henry Rhind, Esq., F.S.A., etc. In large folio, pp. 30 of text, and 16 plates coloured, bound in cloth. 21*s.*

Furnivall.—Education in Early England. Some Notes used as Forewords to a Collection of Treatises on "Manners and Meals in the Olden Time," for the Early English Text Society. By Frederick J. Furnivall, M.A., Trinity Hall, Cambridge, Member of Council of the Philological and Early English Text Societies. 8vo, sewed, pp. 74. 1*s.*

Gesenius' Hebrew Grammar. Translated from the 17th Edition. By Dr. T. J. Conant. With grammatical Exercises and a Chrestomathy by the Translator. 8vo. pp. xvi. and 364, cloth. 10*s.* 6*d.*

Gesenius' Hebrew and English Lexicon of the Old Testament, including the Biblical Chaldee, from the Latin. By Edward Robinson. Fifth Edition. 8vo. pp. xii. and 1160, cloth. 1*l.* 5*s.*

Goldstücker.—A DICTIONARY, SANSKRIT AND ENGLISH, extended and improved from the Second Edition of the Dictionary of Professor H. H. WILSON, with his sanction and concurrence. Together with a Supplement, Grammatical Appendices, and an Index, serving as a Sanskrit-English Vocabulary. By THEODOR GOLDSTÜCKER. Parts I. to VI. 4to. pp. 400. 1856-1863. Each Part 6*s*.

Goldstücker.—A COMPENDIOUS SANSKRIT-ENGLISH DICTIONARY, for the Use of those who intend to read the easier Works of Classical Sanskrit Literature. By THEODOR GOLDSTÜCKER. Small 4to. pp. 900, cloth. [*In preparation.*

Goldstücker.—PANINI: His Place in Sanskrit Literature. An Investigation of some Literary and Chronological Questions which may be settled by a study of his Work. A separate impression of the Preface to the Facsimile of MS. No. 17 in the Library of Her Majesty's Home Government for India, which contains a portion of the MANAVA-KALPA-SUTRA, with the Commentary of KUMARILA-SWAMIN. By THEODOR GOLDSTÜCKER. Imperial 8vo. pp. 268, cloth. 12*s*.

Grammatography.—A MANUAL OF REFERENCE to the Alphabets of Ancient and Modern Languages. Based on the German Compilation of F. BALLHORN. In one volume, royal 8vo. pp. 80, cloth. 7*s*. 6*d*.

The "Grammatography" is offered to the public as a compendious introduction to the reading of the most important ancient and modern languages. Simple in its design, it will be consulted with advantage by the philological student, the amateur linguist, the bookseller, the corrector of the press, and the diligent compositor.

ALPHABETICAL INDEX.

Afghan (or Pushto).	Czechian (or Bohemian).	Hebrew (current hand).	Polish.
Amharic.	Danish.	Hebrew (Judæo-German).	Pushto (or Afghan).
Anglo-Saxon.	Demotic.	Hungarian.	Romaic (Modern Greek)
Arabic.	Estrangelo.	Illyrian.	Russian.
Arabic Ligatures.	Ethiopic.	Irish.	Runes.
Aramaic.	Etruscan.	Italian (Old).	Samaritan.
Archaic Characters.	Georgian.	Japanese.	Sanscrit.
Armenian.	German.	Javanese.	Servian.
Assyrian Cuneiform.	Glagolitic.	Lettish.	Slavonic (Old).
Bengali.	Gothic.	Mantshu.	Sorbian (or Wendish).
Bohemian (Czechian).	Greek.	Median Cuneiform.	Swedish.
Bûgîs.	Greek Ligatures.	Modern Greek (Romaic)	Syriac.
Burmese.	Greek (Archaic).	Mongolian.	Tamil.
Canarese (or Carnâtaca).	Gujerati (or Guzzeratte).	Numidian.	Telugu.
Chinese.	Hieratic.	Old Slavonic (or Cyrillic).	Tibetan.
Coptic.	Hieroglyphics.	Palmyrenian.	Turkish.
Croato-Glagolitic.	Hebrew.	Persian.	Wallachian.
Cufic.	Hebrew (Archaic).	Persian Cuneiform.	Wendish (or Sorbian).
Cyrillic (or Old Slavonic).	Hebrew (Rabbinical).	Phœnician.	Zend.

Grey.—HANDBOOK OF AFRICAN, AUSTRALIAN, AND POLYNESIAN PHILOLOGY, as represented in the Library of His Excellency Sir George Grey, K.C.B., Her Majesty's High Commissioner of the Cape Colony. Classed, Annotated, and Edited by Sir GEORGE GREY and Dr. H. I. BLEEK.

Vol. I. Part 1.—South Africa. 8vo. pp. 186. 7*s*. 6*d*.
Vol. I. Part 2.—Africa (North of the Tropic of Capricorn). 8vo. pp. 70. 2*s*.
Vol. I. Part 3.—Madagascar. 8vo. pp. 24. 1*s*.
Vol. II. Part 1.—Australia. 8vo. pp. iv. and 44. 1*s*. 6*d*.
Vol. II. Part 2.—Papuan Languages of the Loyalty Islands and New Hebrides, comprising those of the Islands of Nengone, Lifu, Aneitum, Tana, and others. 8vo. p. 12. 6*d*.
Vol. II. Part 3.—Fiji Islands and Rotuma (with Supplement to Part II., Papuan Languages, and Part I., Australia). 8vo. pp. 34. 1*s*.
Vol. II. Part 4.—New Zealand, the Chatham Islands, and Auckland Islands. 8vo. pp. 76. 3*s*. 6*d*.
Vol. II. Part 4 (*continuation*).—Polynesia and Borneo. 8vo. pp. 77-154. 3*s*. 6*d*.
Vol. III. Part 1.—Manuscripts and Incunables. 8vo. pp. viii. and 24. 2*s*.
Vol. IV. Part 1.—Early Printed Books. England. 8vo. pp. vi. and 266.

Grey.—MAORI MEMENTOS: being a Series of Addresses presented by the Native People to His Excellency Sir George Grey, K.C.B., F.R.S. With Introductory Remarks and Explanatory Notes; to which is added a small Collection of Laments, etc. By CH. OLIVER B. DAVIS. 8vo. pp. iv. and 228, cloth. 12*s*.

Griffith.—SCENES FROM THE RAMAYANA, MEGHADUTA, ETC. Translated by RALPH T. H. GRIFFITH, M.A. Fcap. 8vo. cloth, pp. 200. 5*s*.

CONTENTS.—Preface—Ayodhya—Ravan Doomed—The Birth of Rama—The Heir apparent—Manthara's Guile—Dasaratha's Oath—The Step-mother—Mother and Son—The Triumph of

Love—Farewell?—The Hermit's Son—The Trial of Truth—The Forest—The Rape of Sita—Rama's Despair—The Messenger Cloud—Khumbakarna—The Suppliant Dove—True Glory—Feed the Poor—The Wise Scholar.

Grout.—THE ISIZULU: a Grammar of the Zulu Language; accompanied with an Historical Introduction, also with an Appendix. By Rev. LEWIS GROUT. 8vo. pp. lii. and 432, cloth. 21*s.*

Haug.—ESSAYS ON THE SACRED LANGUAGE, WRITINGS, AND RELIGION OF THE PARSEES. By MARTIN HAUG, Dr. Phil. Superintendent of Sanskrit Studies in the Poona College. 8vo. pp. 278, cloth. 21*s.*

Haug.—A LECTURE ON AN ORIGINAL SPEECH OF ZOROASTER (Yasna 45), with remarks on his age. By MARTIN HAUG, Ph.D. 8vo. pp. 28, sewed. Bombay, 1865. 2*s.*

Haug.—OUTLINE OF A GRAMMAR OF THE ZEND LANGUAGE. By MARTIN HAUG, Dr. Phil. 8vo. pp. 82, sewed. 14*s.*

Haug.—THE AITAREYA BRAHMANAM OF THE RIG VEDA: containing the Earliest Speculations of the Brahmans on the meaning of the Sacrificial Prayers, and on the Origin, Performance, and Sense of the Rites of the Vedic Religion. Edited, Translated, and Explained by MARTIN HAUG, Ph.D., Superintendent of Sanskrit Studies in the Poona College. etc., etc. In 2 Vols. Crown 8vo. Vol. I. Contents, Sanskrit Text, with Preface, Introductory Essay, and a Map of the Sacrificial Compound at the Soma Sacrifice, pp. 312. Vol. II. Translation with Notes, pp. 544. £2 2*s.*

Haug.—AN OLD ZAND-PAHLAVI GLOSSARY. Edited in the Original Characters, with a Transliteration in Roman Letters, an English Translation, and an Alphabetical Index. By DESTUR HOSHENGJI JAMASPJI, High-priest of the Parsis in Malwa, India. Revised with Notes and Introduction by MARTIN HAUG, Ph.D., late Superintendent of Sanscrit Studies in the Poona College, Foreign Member of the Royal Bavarian Academy. Published by order of the Government of Bombay. 8vo. sewed, pp. lvi. and 132. 15*s.*

Haug.—THE RELIGION OF THE ZOROASTRIANS, as contained in their Sacred Writings. With a History of the Zend and Pehlevi Literature, and a Grammar of the Zend and Pehlevi Languages. By MARTIN HAUG, Ph.D., late Superintendent of Sanscrit Studies in the Poona College. 2 vols. 8vo. [*In preparation.*

Heaviside.—AMERICAN ANTIQUITIES; or, the New World the Old, and the Old World the New. By JOHN T. C. HEAVISIDE. 8vo. pp. 46, sewed. 1*s.* 6*d.*

Hepburn.—A JAPANESE AND ENGLISH DICTIONARY. With an English and Japanese Index. By J. C. HEPBURN, A.M., M.D. Imperial 8vo. cloth, pp. xii., 560 and 132. 5*l.* 5*s.*

Hernisz.—A GUIDE TO CONVERSATION IN THE ENGLISH AND CHINESE LANGUAGES, for the use of Americans and Chinese in California and elsewhere. By STANISLAS HERNISZ. Square 8vo. pp. 274, sewed. 10*s.* 6*d.*

The Chinese characters contained in this work are from the collections of Chinese groups, engraved on steel, and cast into moveable types, by Mr. Marcellin Legrand, engraver of the Imperial Printing Office at Paris. They are used by most of the missions to China.

Hincks.—SPECIMEN CHAPTERS OF AN ASSYRIAN GRAMMAR. By the late Rev. E. HINCKS, D.D., Hon. M. R. A. S. 8vo., pp. 44, sewed. 1*s.*

History of the Sect of Maharajahs; or, VALLABHACHARYAS IN WESTERN INDIA. With a Steel Plate. One Vol. 8vo. pp. 384, cloth. 12*s.*

Hoffmann.—SHOPPING DIALOGUES, in Japanese, Dutch, and English. By Professor J. HOFFMANN. Oblong 8vo. pp. xiii. and 44, sewed. 3*s.*

Howse.—A GRAMMAR OF THE CREE LANGUAGE. With which is combined an analysis of the Chippeway Dialect. By JOSEPH HOWSE, Esq., F.R.G.S. 8vo. pp. xx. and 324, cloth. 7*s.* 6*d.*

Hunter.—A COMPARATIVE DICTIONARY OF THE LANGUAGES OF INDIA AND HIGH ASIA, with a Dissertation, based on The Hodgson Lists, Official Records, and Manuscripts. By W. W. HUNTER, B.A., M.R.A.S., Honorary Fellow Ethnological Society, of Her Majesty's Bengal Civil Service. Folio, pp. vi. and 224, cloth. £2 2*s.*

Ikhwánu-s Safá.—IHKWÁNU-S SAFÁ; or, BROTHERS OF PURITY. Describing the Contention between Men and Beasts as to the Superiority of the Human Race. Translated from the Hindustání by Professor J. DOWSON, Staff College, Sandhurst. Crown 8vo. pp. viii. and 156, cloth. 7*s.*

Inman.—ANCIENT FAITHS EMBODIED IN ANCIENT TIMES; or, an attempt to trace the Religious Belief, Sacred Rites, and Holy Emblems of certain Nations, by an interpretation of the Names given to Children by pristly authority, or assumed by prophets, kings and hierarchs. By THOMAS INMAN, M.D., Liverpool. Vol. I. 8vo. cloth, pp. viii. and 800. 30*s.* [Vol. 2 *nearly ready.*

Jaeschke.—A SHORT PRACTICAL GRAMMAR OF THE TIBETAN LANGUAGE, with special Reference to the Spoken Dialects. By H. A. JAESCHKE, Moravian Missionary. 8vo. sewed, pp. ii. and 56.

Jaeschke.—ROMANIZED TIBETAN AND ENGLISH DICTIONARY, each word being re-produced in the Tibetan as well as in the Roman character. By H. A. JAESCHKE, Moravian Missionary. 8vo. pp. ii. and 158, sewed. 5*s.*

Justi.—HANDBUCH DER ZENDSPRACHE, VON FERDINAND JUSTI. Altbactrisches Woerterbuch. Grammatik Chrestomathie. Four parts, 4to. sewed, pp. xxii. and 424. Leipzig, 1864. 24*s.*

Kafir Essays, and other Pieces; with an English Translation. Edited by the Right Rev. the BISHOP OF GRAHAMSTOWN. 32mo. pp. 84, sewed. 2*s* 6*d.*

Kalidasa.—RAGHUVANSA. By KALIDASA. No. 1. (Cantos 1-3.) With Notes and Grammatical Explanations, by Rev. K. M. BANERJEA, Second Professor of Bishop's College, Calcutta; Member of the Board of Examiners, Fort-William; Honorary Member of the Royal Asiatic Society, London. 8vo. sewed, pp. 70. 4*s.* 6*d.*

Khirad-Afroz (The Illuminator of the Understanding). By Maulaví Hafízu'd-dín. A new edition of the Hindústání Text, carefully revised, with Notes, Critical and Explanatory. By EDWARD B. EASTWICK, F.R.S., F.S.A., M.R.A.S., Professor of Hindústání at the late East India Company's College at Haileybury. 8vo. cloth, pp. xiv. and 321. 18*s.*

Kidd.—CATALOGUE OF THE CHINESE LIBRARY OF THE ROYAL ASIATIC SOCIETY. By the Rev. S. KIDD. 8vo. pp. 58, sewed. 1*s.*

Laghu Kaumudí. A Sanskrit Grammar. By Varadarája. With an English Version, Commentary, and References. By JAMES R. BALLANTYNE, LL.D., Principal of the Sanskrit College, Benares. 8vo. pp. xxxvi. and 424, cloth. £1 11*s.* 6*d.*

Legge.—THE CHINESE CLASSICS. With a Translation, Critical and Exegetical, Notes, Prolegomena, and Copious Indexes. By JAMES LEGGE, D.D., of the London Missionary Society. In seven vols. Vol. I. containing Confucian Analects, the Great Learning, and the Doctrine of the Mean. 8vo. pp. 526, cloth. £2 2*s.*—Vol. II., containing the Works of Mencius. 8vo. pp. 634, cloth. £2 2*s.*—Vol. III. Part I. containing the First Part of the Shoo-King, or the Books of T. Aug, the Books of Yu, the Books of Hea, the Books of Shang, and the Prolegomena. Royal 8vo. pp. viii. and 280, cloth. £2 2*s.*—Vol. III. Part II. containing the Fifth Part of the Shoo-King, or the Books of Chow, and the Indexes. Royal 8vo. pp. 281—736, cloth. £2 2*s.*

Legge.—THE LIFE AND TEACHINGS OF CONFUCIUS, with Explanatory Notes. By JAMES LEGGE, D.D. Reproduced for General Readers from the Author's work, "The Chinese Classics," with the original Text. Second edition. Crown 8vo. cloth, pp. vi. and 338. 10*s.* 6*d.*

Leitner.—THE RACES AND LANGUAGES OF DARDISTAN. By G. W. LEITNER, M.A., Ph.D., Honorary Fellow of King's College London, etc.; late on Special Duty in Kashmir. 4 vols. 4to. [*In the press.*

Leland.—HANS BREITMANN'S PARTY. With other Ballads. By CHARLES G. LELAND. Eighth Edition. Square, pp. xvi. and 74, sewed. 1*s.*

Leland.—HANS BREITMANN'S CHRISTMAS. With other Ballads. By CHARLES G. LELAND. Second edition. Square, pp. 80, sewed. 1*s.*

Leland.—HANS BREITMANN AS A POLITICIAN. By CHARLES G. LELAND. Second edition. Square, pp. 72, sewed. 1*s*.

Lesley.—MAN'S ORIGIN AND DESTINY, Sketched from the Platform of the Sciences, in a Course of Lectures delivered before the Lowell Institute, in Boston, in the Winter of 1865-6. By J. P. LESLEY, Member of the National Academy of the United States, Secretary of the American Philosophical Society. Numerous Woodcuts. Crown 8vo. pp. 392, cloth. 10*s*. 6*d*.

CONTENTS.—Lecture 1. On the Classification of the Sciences; 2. On the Genius of the Physical Sciences, Ancient and Modern; 3. The Geological Antiquity of Man; 4. On the Dignity of Mankind; 5. On the Unity of Mankind; 6. On the Early Social Life of Man; 7. On Language as a Test of Race; 8. The Origin of Architecture; 9. The Growth of the Alphabet; 10. The Four Types of Religious Worship; 11. On Arkite Symbolism. Appendix.

Lobscheid.—ENGLISH AND CHINESE DICTIONARY, with the Punti and Mandarin Pronunciation. By the Rev. W. LOBSCHEID, Knight of Francis Joseph, C.M.I.R.G.S.A., N.Z.B.S.V., etc. Folio, pp. viii. and 2016, bound in 2 vols., cloth. £7 10*s*.

Ludewig (Hermann E.)—The LITERATURE of AMERICAN ABORIGINAL LANGUAGES. With Additions and Corrections by Professor WM. W. TURNER. Edited by NICOLAS TRÜBNER. 8vo. fly and general Title, 2 leaves; Dr. Ludewig's Preface, pp. v.—viii.; Editor's Preface, pp. iv.—xii.; Biographical Memoir of Dr. Ludewig, pp. xiii.—xiv.; and Introductory Biographical Notices, pp. xiv.—xxiv., followed by List of Contents. Then follow Dr. Ludewig's Bibliotheca Glottica, alphabetically arranged, with Additions by the Editor, pp. 1—209; Professor Turner's Additions, with those of the Editor to the same, also alphabetically arranged, pp. 210—246; Index, pp. 247—256; and List of Errata, pp. 257, 258. One vol. handsomely bound in cloth. 10*s*. 6*d*.

Manava-Kalpa-Sutra; being a portion of this ancient Work on Vaidik Rites, together with the Commentary of KUMARILA-SWAMIN. A Facsimile of the MS. No. 17, in the Library of Her Majesty's Home Government for India. With a Preface by THEODOR GOLDSTÜCKER. Oblong folio, pp. 268 of letter-press and 121 leaves of facsimiles. Cloth. £4 4*s*.

Manipulus Vocabulorum; A Rhyming Dictionary of the English Language. By Peter Levins (1570) Edited, with an Alphabetical Index by HENRY B. WHEATLEY. 8vo. pp. xvi. and 370, cloth. 14*s*.

Manning.—AN INQUIRY INTO THE CHARACTER AND ORIGIN OF THE POSSESSIVE AUGMENT in English and in Cognate Dialects. By JAMES MANNING, Q.A.S., Recorder of Oxford. 8vo. pp. iv. and 90. 2*s*.

Markham.—QUICHUA GRAMMAR and DICTIONARY. Contributions towards a Grammar and Dictionary of Quichua, the Language of the Yncas of Peru; collected by CLEMENTS R. MARKHAM, F.S.A., Corr. Mem. of the University of Chile. Author of "Cuzco and Lima," and "Travels in Peru and India." In one vol. crown 8vo., pp. 223, cloth. 10*s*. 6*d*.

Mason.—BURMAH: its People and Natural Productions; or Notes on the Nations, Fauna, Flora, and Minerals of Tenasserim, Pegu, and Burmah; with Systematic Catalogues of the known Mammals, Birds, Fish, Reptiles, Mollusks, Crustaceans, Annalids, Radiates, Plants, and Minerals, with Vernacular names. By Rev. F. MASON, D.D., M.R.A.S., Corresponding Member of the American Oriental Society, of the Boston Society of Natural History, and of the Lyceum of Natural History, New York. 8vo. pp. xviii. and 914, cloth. Rangoon, 1860. 30*s*.

Mason.—A PALI GRAMMAR, on the Basis of Kachchayano. With Chrestomathy and Vocabulary. By FRANCIS MASON, D.D., M.R.A.S. and American Oriental Society. 8vo. sewed, pp. iv., viii., and 214, 31*s*. 6*d*.

Mathuraprasada Misra.—A TRILINGUAL DICTIONARY, being a comprehensive Lexicon in English, Urdú, and Hindí, exhibiting the Syllabication-Pronunciation, and Etymology of English Words, with their Explanation in English, and in Urdú and Hindí in the Roman Character. By MATHURÁ, PRASÁDA MISRA, Second Master, Queen's College, Benares. 8vo. pp. xiv. and 1330, cloth. Benares, 1865. £2 2*s*.

Medhurst.—CHINESE DIALOGUES, QUESTIONS, and FAMILIAR SENTENCES, literally translated into English, with a view to promote commercial intercourse and assist beginners in the Language. By the late W. H. MEDHURST, D.D. A new and enlarged Edition. 8vo. pp. 226. 18*s*.

Megha-Duta (The). (Cloud-Messenger.) By Kālidāsa. Translated from the Sanskrit into English verse, with Notes and Illustrations. By the late H. H. WILSON, M.A., F.R.S., Boden Professor of Sanskrit in the University of Oxford, etc., etc. The Vocabulary by FRANCIS JOHNSON, sometime Professor of Oriental Languages at the College of the Honourable the East India Company, Haileybury. New Edition. 4to. cloth, pp. xi. and 180. 10*s*. 6*d*.

Memoirs read before the ANTHROPOLOGICAL SOCIETY OF LONDON, 1863-1864. In one volume, 8vo., pp. 542, cloth. 21*s*.

CONTENTS.—I. On the Negro's Place in Nature. By James Hunt, Ph.D., F.S.A., F.R.S.L. F.A.S.L., President of the Anthropological Society of London.—II. On the Weight of the Brain in the Negro. By Thomas B. Peacock, M.D., F.R.C.P., F.A.S.L.—III. Observations on the Past and Present Populations of the New World. By W. Bollaert, Esq., F.A.S.L.—IV. On the Two Principal Forms of Ancient British and Gaulish Skulls. By J. Thurnam, Esq., M.D., F.A.S.L. With Lithographic Plates and Woodcuts.—V. Introduction to the Palæography of America; or, Observations on Ancient Picture and Figurative Writing in the New World; on the Fictitious Writing in North America; on the Quipu of the Peruvians, and Examination of Spurious Quipus. By William Bollaert, Esq., F.A.S.L.—VI. Viti and its Inhabitants. By W. T. Pritchard, Esq., F.R.G.S., F.A.S.L.—VII. On the Astronomy of the Red Man of the New World. By W. Bollaert, Esq., F.A.S.L.—VIII. The Neanderthal Skull: its peculiar formation considered anatomically. By J. Barnard Davis, M.D., F.S.A., F.A.S.L.—IX. On the Discovery of large Kist-vaens on the "Muckle Heog," in the Island of Unst (Shetland), containing Urns of Chloritic Schist. By George E. Roberts, Esq., F.G.S., Hon. Sec. A.S.L. With Notes on the Human Remains. By C. Carter Blake, Esq., F.A.S.L., F.G.S.—X. Notes on some Facts connected with the Dahoman. By Capt. Richard F. Burton, V.P.A.S.L.—XI. On certain Anthropological Matters connected with the South Sea Islanders (the Samoans). By W. T. Pritchard, Esq., F.R.G.S., F.A.S.L.—XII. On the Phallic Worship of India. By Edward Sellon.—XIII. The History of Anthropology. By T. Bendyshe, M.A., F.A.S.L., Vice-President A.S.L.—XIV. On the Two Principal Forms of Ancient British and Gaulish Skulls. Part II. with Appendix of Tables of Measurement. By John Thurnam, M.D., F.S.A., F.A.S.L.—APPENDIX. On the Weight of the Brain and Capacity of the Cranial Cavity of the Negro. By Thomas B. Peacock, M.D., F.R.C.P., F.A.S.L.

Memoirs read before the ANTHROPOLOGICAL SOCIETY OF LONDON, 1865-6. Vol. II. 8vo. pp. x. 464, cloth. London, 1866. 21*s*.

CONTENTS.—I. The Difference between the Larynx of the White Man and Negro. By Dr. Gibb.—II. On the Dervishes of the East. By Arminius Vambery.—III. Origin and Customs of the Gallinas of Sierra Leone. By J. Meyer Harris.—IV. On the Permanence of Anthropological Types. By Dr. Beddoe.—V. The Maya Alphabet. By Wm. Ballaert.—VI. The People of Spain. By H. J. C. Beavan.—VII. Genealogy and Anthropology. By G. M. Marshall.—VIII. Simious Skulls. By C. Carter Blake.—IX. A New Goniometer. By Dr. Paul Broca.—X. Anthropology of the New World. By Wm. Bollaert.—XI. On the Psychical Characteristics of the English. By Luke Owen Pike.—XII. Iconography of the Skull. By W. H. Wesley.—XIII. Orthographic Projection of the Skull. By A. Higgins.—XIV. On Hindu Neology. By Major S. R. I. Owen.—XV. The Brochs of Orkney. By George Petrie.—XVI. Ancient Caithness Remains. By Jos. Anderson.—XVII. Description of Living Microcephale. By Dr. Shortt.—XVIII. Notes on an Hermaphrodite. By Captain Burton.—XIX. On the Sacti Puja. By E. Sellon.—XX. Resemblance of Inscriptions on British and American Rocks. By Dr. Seemann.—XXI. Sterility of the Union of White and Black Races. By R. B. N. Walker.—XXII. Analogous Forms of Flint Implements. By H. M. Westropp.—XXIII. Explorations in Unst, Brassay, and Zetland. By Dr. Hunt, President.—XXIV. Report of Expedition to Zetland. By Ralph Tate.—XXV. The Head-forms of the West of England. By Dr. Beddoe.—XXVI. Explorations in the Kirkhead Cave at Ulverstone. By J. P. Morris.—XXVII. On the Influence of Peat on the Human Body. By Dr. Hunt.—XXVIII. On Stone Inscriptions in the Island of Brassay. By Dr. Hunt.—XXIX. The History of Ancient Slavery. By Dr. John Bower.—XXX. Blood Relationship in Marriage. By Dr. Arthur Mitchell.

Merx.—GRAMMATICA SYRIACA, quam post opus Hoffmanni refecit ADALBERTUS MERX, Phil. Dr. Theol. Lic. in Univ. Litt. Jenensi Priv. Docens. Particula I. Royal 8vo. sewed, pp. 136. 7*s*.

Moffat.—THE STANDARD ALPHABET PROBLEM; or the Preliminary Subject of a General Phonic System, considered on the basis of some important facts in the Sechwana Language of South Africa, and in reference to the views of Professors Lepsius, Max Müller, and others. A contribution to Phonetic Philology. By ROBERT MOFFAT, junr., Surveyor, Fellow of the Royal Geographical Society. 8vo. pp. xxviii. and 174, cloth. 7*s*. 6*d*.

Molesworth.—A DICTIONARY, MÁRATHI and ENGLISH. Compiled by J. T. MOLESWORTH, assisted by GEORGE and THOMAS CANDY. Second Edition, revised and enlarged. By J. T. MOLESWORTH. Royal 4to. pp. xxx and 922, boards. Bombay, 1857. £3 3*s*.

Morley.—A DESCRIPTIVE CATALOGUE of the HISTORICAL MANUSCRIPTS in the ARABIC and PERSIAN LANGUAGES preserved in the Library of the Royal Asiatic Society of Great Britain and Ireland. By WILLIAM H. MORLEY, M.R.A.S. 8vo. pp. viii. and 160, sewed. London, 1854. 2*s*. 6*d*.

Morrison.—A DICTIONARY OF THE CHINESE LANGUAGE. By the Rev. R. MORRISON, D.D. Two vols. Vol. I. pp. x. and 762; Vol. II. pp. 828, cloth. Shanghae, 1865. £4 4*s*.

Muhammed.—THE LIFE OF MUHAMMED. Based on Muhammed Ibn Ishak. By Abd El Malik Ibn Hisham. Edited by Dr. FERDINAND WÜSTENFIELD. One volume containing the Arabic Text. 8vo. pp. 1026, sewed. Price 21*s*. Another volume, containing Introduction, Notes, and Index in German. 8vo. pp. lxxii. and 266, sewed. 7*s*. 6*d*. Each part sold separately.

The test based on the Manuscripts of the Berlin, Leipsic, Gotha and Leyden Libraries, has been carefully revised by the learned editor, and printed with the utmost exactness.

Muir.—ORIGINAL SANSKRIT TEXTS, on the Origin and History of the People of India, their Religion and Institutions. Collected, Translated and Illustrated by JAMES MUIR, Esq., D.C.L., LL.D. Vol. I.: Mythical and Legendary Accounts of the Origin of Caste, with an Enquiry into its existence in the Vedic Age. Second edition, re-written and greatly enlarged. In 1 vol. 8vo. pp. xx, 532, cloth. 21*s*.

Muir.—ORIGINAL SANSKRIT TEXTS, on the Origin and History of the People of India, their Religion and Institutions. Collected, Translated, and Illustrated, by J. MUIR, Esq., D.C.L., LL.D., Ph.D., Bonn. Volume III., The Vedas: Opinions of their Authors, and of later Indian Writers, on their Origin, Inspiration, and Authority. Second edition, enlarged. 8vo. pp. xxxii. and 312, cloth. 16*s*.

Muir.—ORIGINAL SANSKRIT TEXTS on the Origin and History of the People of India, their Religion and Institutions. Collected, Translated into English, and Illustrated by Remarks. By J. MUIR, Esq., D.C.L., LL.D. Vol. IV. Comparison of the Vedic with the later representation of the principal Indian Deities. 8vo. pp. xii. and 440, cloth. 15*s*. [*A New Edition of Vol. II. is in preparation.*

Müller.—THE SACRED HYMNS OF THE BRAHMINS, as preserved to us in the oldest collection of religious poetry, the Rig-Veda-Sanhita, translated and explained. By F. MAX MÜLLER, M.A., Taylorian Professor of Modern European Languages in the University of Oxford, Fellow of All Souls' College. In 8 vols. Volume I. 8vo. pp. clii. and 264. 12*s*. 6*d*.

Newman.—A HANDBOOK OF MODERN ARABIC, consisting of a Practical Grammar, with numerous Examples, Dialogues, and Newspaper Extracts, in a European Type. By F. W. NEWMAN, Emeritus Professor of University College, London; formerly Fellow of Balliol College, Oxford. Post 8vo. pp. xx. and 192, cloth. London, 1866. 6*s*.

Newman.—THE TEXT OF THE IGUVINE INSCRIPTIONS, with interlinear Latin Translation and Notes. By FRANCIS W. NEWMAN, late Professor of Latin at University College, London. 8vo. pp. xvi. and 54, sewed. 2*s*.

Notley.—A COMPARATIVE GRAMMAR OF THE FRENCH, ITALIAN, SPANISH, AND PORTUGUESE LANGUAGES. By EDWIN A. NOTLEY. Crown oblong 8vo. cloth, pp. xv. and 396. 10*s*. 6*d*.

Oriental Text Society.

The Publications of the Oriental Text Society.

1. THEOPHANIA; or, Divine Manifestations of our Lord and Saviour. By EUSEBIUS, Bishop of Cæsarea. Syriac. Edited by Prof. S. LEE. 8vo. 1842. 15*s*.
2. ATHANASIUS'S FESTAL LETTERS, discovered in an ancient Syriac Version. Edited by the Rev. W. CURETON. 8vo. 1848. 15*s*.
3. SHAHRASTANI: Book of Religious and Philosophical Sects, in Arabic. Two Parts. 8vo. 1842. 30*s*.
4. UMDAT AKIDAT AHL AL SUNNAT WA AL TAMAAT; Pillar of the Creed of the Sunnites. Edited in Arabic by the Rev. W. CURETON. 8vo. 1843. 5*s*.

Oriental Text Society's Publications *continued.*

5. HISTORY OF THE ALMOHADES. Edited in Arabic by Dr. R. P. A. DOZY. 8vo. 1847. 10*s.* 6*d.*
6. SAMA VEDA. Edited in Sanskrit by Rev. G. STEVENSON. 8vo. 1843. 12*s.*
7. DASA KUMARA CHARITA. Edited in Sanskrit by Professor H. H. WILSON. 8vo. 1846. £1 4*s.*
8. MAHA VIRA CHARITA, or a History of Rama. A Sanskrit Play. Edited by F. H. TRITHEN. 8vo. 1848. 15*s.*
9. MAKHZAN UL ASRAR: The Treasury of Secrets. By NIZAMI. Edited in Persian by N. BLAND. 4to. 1844. 10*s.* 6*d.*
10. SALAMAN-U-UBSAL; A Romance of Jami (Dshami). Edited in Persian by F. FALCONER. 4to. 1843. 10*s.*
11. MIRKHOND'S HISTORY OF THE ATABEKS. Edited in Persian by W. H. MORLEY. 8vo. 1850. 12*s.*
12. TUHFAT-UL-AHRAR; the Gift of the Noble. A Poem. By Jami (Dshami). Edited in Persian by F. FALCONER. 4to. 1843. 10*s.*

Osburn.—THE MONUMENTAL HISTORY of EGYPT, as recorded on the Ruins of her Temples, Palaces, and Tombs. By WILLIAM OSBURN. Illustrated with Maps, Plates, etc. 2 vols. 8vo. pp. xii. and 461; vii. and 643, cloth. £2 2*s.*
Vol. I.—From the Colonization of the Valley to the Visit of the Patriarch Abram.
Vol. II.—From the Visit of Abram to the Exodus.

Palmer.—EGYPTIAN CHRONICLES, with a harmony of Sacred and Egyptian Chronology, and an Appendix on Babylonian and Assyrian Antiquities. By WILLIAM PALMER, M.A., and late Fellow of Magdalen College, Oxford. 2 vols., 8vo. cloth, pp. lxxiv. and 428, and viii. and 636. 1861. 12*s.*

Patell.—COWASJEE PATELL'S CHRONOLOGY, containing corresponding Dates of the different Eras used by Christians, Jews, Greeks, Hindús, Mohamedans, Parsees, Chinese, Japanese, etc. By COWASJEE SORABJEE PATELL. 4to. pp. viii. and 184, cloth. 50*s.*

Percy.—BISHOP PERCY'S FOLIO MANUSCRIPTS—BALLADS AND ROMANCES. Edited by John W. Hales, M.A., Fellow and late Assistant Tutor of Christ's College, Cambridge; and Frederick J. Furnivall, M.A., of Trinity Hall, Cambridge; assisted by Professor Child, of Harvard University, Cambridge, U.S.A., W. Chappell, Esq., etc. In 3 volumes. Vol. I., pp. 610; Vol. 2, pp. 681.; Vol. 3, pp. 640. Demy 8vo. half-bound, 2*l.* 2*s.* Extra demy 8vo. half-bound, on Whatman's ribbed paper, 3*l.* 15*s.* Extra royal 8vo., paper covers, on Whatman's best ribbed paper, 7*l.* 17*s.* 6*d.* Large 4to. paper covers, on Whatman's best ribbed paper, 15*l.* 15*s.*

Perrin.—ENGLISH ZULU DICTIONARY. New Edition, revised by J. A. BRICKHILL, Interpreter to the Supreme Court of Natal. 12mo. pp. 226, cloth, Pietermaritzburg, 1865. 5*s.*

Philological Society.—PROPOSALS for the Publication of a NEW ENGLISH DICTIONARY. 8vo. pp. 32, sewed. 6*d.*

Pierce the Ploughman's Crede (about 1394 Anno Domini). Transcribed and Edited from Manuscripts of Trinity College, Cambridge, R. 3, 15. Collated with Manuscripts Bibl. Reg. 18. B. xvii. in the British Museum, and with the old Printed Text of 1553, to which is appended "God spede the Plough" (about 1500 Anno Domini). From Manuscripts Landsdowne, 762. By the Rev. WALTER W. SKEAT, M.A., late Fellow of Christ's College, Cambridge. pp. xx. and 75, cloth. 1867. 2*s.* 6*d.*

Prakrita-Prakasa; or, The Prakrit Grammar of Vararuchi, with the Commentary (Manorama) of Bhamaha. The first complete edition of the Original Text with Various Readings from a Collation of Six Manuscripts in the Bodleian Library at Oxford, and the Libraries of the Royal Asiatic Society and the East India House; with copious Notes, an English Translation, and Index of Prakrit words, to which is prefixed an easy Introduction to Prakrit Grammar. By EDWARD BYLES COWELL, of Magdalen Hall, Oxford, Professor of Sanskrit at Cambridge. Second issue, with new Preface, and corrections. In 1 vol. 8vo. pp. xxxii. and 204. 14*s.*

Priaulx.—Quæstiones Mosaicæ; or, the first part of the Book of Genesis compared with the remains of ancient religions. By Osmond de Beauvoir Priaulx. 8vo. pp. viii. and 548, cloth. 12*s.*

Raja-Niti.—A Collection of Hindu Apologues, in the Braj Bháshá Language. Revised edition. With a Preface, Notes, and Supplementary Glossary. By Fitzedward Hall, Esq. 8vo. cloth, pp. 204. 21*s.*

Ram Raz.—Essay on the Architecture of the Hindus. By Ram Raz, Native Judge and Magistrate of Bangalore, Corresponding Member of the R.A.S. of Great Britain and Ireland. With 48 plates. 4to. pp. xiv. and 64, sewed. London, 1834. Original selling price, £1 11*s.* 6*d.*, reduced (for a short time only) to 12*s.*

Rask.—A Grammar of the Anglo-Saxon Tongue. From the Danish of Erasmus Rask, Professor of Literary History in, and Librarian to, the University of Copenhagen, etc. By Benjamin Thorpe, Member of the Munich Royal Academy of Sciences, and of the Society of Netherlandish Literature, Leyden. Second edition, corrected and improved. 18mo. pp. 200, cloth. 5*s.* 6*d.*

Rawlinson.—A Commentary on the Cuneiform Inscriptions of Babylonia and Assyria, including Readings of the Inscription on the Nimrud Obelisk, and Brief Notice of the Ancient Kings of Nineveh and Babylon, Read before the Royal Asiatic Society, by Major H. C. Rawlinson. 8vo., pp. 84, sewed. London, 1850. 2*s.* 6*d.*

Rawlinson.—Outlines of Assyrian History, from the Inscriptions of Nineveh. By Lieut. Col. Rawlinson, C.B., followed by some Remarks by A. H. Layard, Esq., D.C.L. 8vo., pp. xliv., sewed. London, 1852. 1*s.*

Renan.—An Essay on the Age and Antiquity of the Book of Nabathæan Agriculture. To which is added an Inaugural Lecture on the Position of the Shemitic Nations in the History of Civilization. By M. Ernest Renan, Membre de l'Institut. In 1 vol., crown 8vo., pp. xvi. and 148, cloth. 3*s.* 6*d.*

Ridley.—Kamilaroi, Dippil, and Turrubul. Languages Spoken by Australian Aborigines. By Rev. Wm. Ridley, M.A., of the University of Sydney; Minister of the Presbyterian Church of New South Wales. Printed by authority. Small 4to. cloth, pp. vi. and 90. 30*s.*

Rig-Veda-Sanhita (The). The Sacred Hymns of the Brahmins, as preserved to us in the oldest collection of Religious Poetry. The Rig-Veda-Sanhita, translated and explained. By F. Max Müller, M.A., Taylorian Professor of Modern European Languages in the University of Oxford, Fellow of All Soul's College. In 8 vols. Vol. I. 8vo. pp. clii. and 264. 12*s.* 6*d.*

[*Vol. I. in the press.*

Rig-Veda Sanhita.—A Collection of Ancient Hindu Hymns. Constituting the First Ashtaka, or Book of the Rig-veda; the oldest authority for the religious and social institutions of the Hindus. Translated from the Original Sanskrit. By the late H. H. Wilson, M.A., F.R.S., etc. etc. etc. Second Edition, with a Postscript by Dr. Fitzedward Hall. Vol. I. 8vo. cloth, pp. lii. and 348, price 21*s.*

Rig-veda Sanhita.—A Collection of Ancient Hindu Hymns, constituting the Fifth to Eighth Ashtakas, or books of the Rig-Veda, the oldest Authority for the Religious and Social Institutions of the Hindus. Translated from the Original Sanskrit by the late Horace Hayman Wilson, M.A., F.R.S., etc. Edited by E. B. Cowell, M.A., Principal of the Calcutta Sanskrit College. Vol. IV., 8vo., pp. 214, cloth. 14*s.*

A few copies of Vols. II. and III. still left. [*V. and VI. in the press.*

Schele de Vere.—Studies in English; or, Glimpses of the Inner Life of our Language. By M. Schele de Vere, LL.D., Professor of Modern Languages in the University of Virginia. 8vo. cloth, pp. vi. and 365. 10*s.* 6*d.*

Schlagintweit.—Buddhism in Tibet. Illustrated by Literary Documents and Objects of Religious Worship. With an Account of the Buddhist Systems preceding it in India. By Emil Schlagintweit, LL.D. With a Folio Atlas of 20 Plates, and 20 Tables of Native Prints in the Text. Royal 8vo., pp. xxiv. and 404. £2 2*s.*

Schlagintweit.—Glossary of Geographical Terms from India and Tibet, with Native Transcription and Transliteration. By Hermann de Schlagintweit. Forming, with a "Route Book of the Western Himalaya, Tibet, and Turkistan," the Third Volume of H., A., and R. de Schlagintweit's "Results of a Scientific Mission to India and High Asia." With an Atlas in imperial folio, of Maps, Panoramas, and Views. Royal 4to., pp. xxiv. and 293. £4.

Shápurjí Edaljí.—A Grammar of the Gujarátí Language. By Shápurjí Edaljí. Cloth, pp. 127. 10*s.* 6*d.*

Shápurjí Edaljí.—A Dictionary, Gujarati and English. By Shápurjí Edaljí. Second Edition. Crown 8vo. cloth, pp. xxiv. and 874. 21*s.*

Sherring.—The Sacred City of the Hindus. An Account of Benares in Ancient and Modern Times. By the Rev. M. A. Sherring, M.A., LL.D.; and Prefaced with an Introduction by Fitzedward Hall, Esq., D.C.L. 8vo. cloth, pp. xxxvi. and 388, with numerous full-page illustrations. 21*s.*

Sophocles.—A Glossary of Later and Byzantine Greek. By E. A. Sophocles. 4to., pp. iv. and 624, cloth. £2 2*s.*

Sophocles.—Romaic or Modern Greek Grammar. By E. A. Sophocles. 8vo. pp. xxviii. and 196. 7*s.* 6*d.*

Stratmann.—A Dictionary of the English Language. Compiled from the writings of the xiiith, xivth, and xvth centuries. By Francis Henry Stratmann. 8vo. cloth, pp. x. and 694. 25*s.*

Stratmann.—An Old English Poem of the Owl and the Nightingale. Edited by Francis Henry Stratmann. 8vo. cloth, pp. 60. 3*s.*

The Boke of Nurture. By John Russell, about 1460–1470 Anno Domini. The Boke of Kernynge. By Wynkyn de Worde, Anno Domini 1513. The Boke of Nurture. By Hugh Rhodes, Anno Domini 1577. Edited from the Originals in the British Museum Library, by Frederick J. Furnivall, M.A., Trinity Hall, Cambridge, Member of Council of the Philological and Early English Text Societies. 4to. half-morocco, gilt top, pp. xix. and 146, 28, xxviii. and 56. 1867. 1*l.* 11*s.* 6*d.*

The Vision of William concerning Piers Plowman, together with Vita de Dowel, Dobet et Dobest, secundum wit et resoun. By William Langland (about 1362-1380 anno domini). Edited from numerous Manuscripts, with Prefaces, Notes, and a Glossary. By the Rev. Walter W. Skeat, M.A. pp. xliv. and 158, cloth, 1867. Vernon Text; Text A. 7*s.* 6*d.*

Thomas.—A Collection of some of the Miscellaneous Essays on Oriental Subjects, published on various occasions. By Edward Thomas, Esq., late of the East India Company's Bengal Civil Service. Very few copies only of this Collection remain unsold. In one volume, 8vo. half-bound.

Contents.—On Ancient Indian Weights.—The Earliest Indian Coinage.—Bactrian Coins.—On the Identity of Xandrames and Kranada.—Note on Indian Numerals.—On the Coins of the Gupta Dynasty—Early Armenian Coins—Observations Introductory to the Explanation of the Oriental Legends to be found on certain Imperial and Partho-Persian Coins—Sassanian Gems and early Armenian Coins.—Notes on certain unpublished Coins of the Sassanidæ.—An account of Eight Kufic Coins—Supplementary Contributions to the Series of the Coins of the Kings of Ghazni—Supplementary Contributions to the Series of the Coins of the Patan Sultans of Hindustan.—The Initial Coinage of Bengal, introduced by the Muhammadans on the conquest of the country, A.H. 600-800, A.D. 1203-1397.

Thomas.—Early Sassanian Inscriptions, Seals and Coins, illustrating the Early History of the Sassanian Dynasty, containing Proclamations of Ardeshir Babek, Sapor I., and his Successors. With a Critical Examination and Explanation of the Celebrated Inscription in the Hájíábad Cave, demonstrating that Sapor, the Conqueror of Valerian, was a Professing Christian. By Edward Thomas, Esq. 8vo. cloth, pp 148, Illustrated 7*s.* 6*d.*

Tindall.—A Grammar and Vocabulary of the Namaqua-Hottentot Language. By Henry Tindall, Wesleyan Missionary. 8vo., pp. 124, sewed. 6*s.*

Van der Tuuk.—Outlines of a Grammar of the Malagasy Language. By H. N. van der Tuuk. 8vo., pp. 28, sewed. 1*s.*

Van der Tuuk.—SHORT ACCOUNT OF THE MALAY MANUSCRIPTS BELONGING TO THE ROYAL ASIATIC SOCIETY. By H N. VAN DER TUUK. 8vo., pp. 52, 2*s*. 6*d*.

Vishnu-Purana (The); a System of Hindu Mythology and Tradition. Translated from the original Sanskrit, and Illustrated by Notes derived chiefly from other Purāṇas. By the late H. H. WILSON, M.A., F.R.S., Boden Professor of Sanskrit in the University of Oxford, etc., etc. Edited by FITZEDWARD HALL. In 6 vols. 8vo. Vol. I. pp. cxl. and 200; Vol. II. pp. 343; Vol. III. pp. 348: Vol. IV., pp. 346 cloth. Price 10*s*. 6*d*. each.

[*Vols. V. and VI. in the press.*

Wade.—YÜ-YEN TZŬ-ERH CHI. A progressive course designed to assist the Student of Colloquial Chinese, as spoken in the Capital and the Metropolitan Department. In eight parts, with Key, Syllabary, and Writing Exercises. By THOMAS FRANCIS WADE, C.B., Secretary to Her Britannic Majesty's Legation, Peking. 3 vols. 4to. Progressive Course, pp. xx. 296 and 16; Syllabary, pp. 126 and 36; Writing Exercises, pp. 48; Key, pp. 174 and 140, sewed. £4.

Wade.—WÊN-CHIEN TZŬ-ERH CHI. A series of papers selected as specimens of documentary Chinese, designed to assist Students of the language, as written by the officials of China. In sixteen parts, with Key. Vol. I. By THOMAS FRANCIS WADE, C.B., Secretary to Her Britannic Majesty's Legation at Peking. 4to., half-cloth, pp. xii. and 455; and iv, 72, and 52. £1 16*s*.

Wake.—CHAPTERS ON MAN. With the Outlines of a Science of comparative Psychology. By C. STANILAND WAKE, Fellow of the Anthropological Society of London. Crown 8vo. pp. viii. and 344, cloth. 7*s*. 6*d*.

Watson.—INDEX TO THE NATIVE AND SCIENTIFIC NAMES OF INDIAN AND OTHER EASTERN ECONOMIC PLANTS AND PRODUCTS, originally prepared under the authority of the Secretary of State for India in Council. By JOHN FORBES WATSON, M.A., M.D., F.L.S., F.R.A.S., etc., Reporter on the Products of India. Imperial 8vo., cloth, pp. 650. £1 11*s*. 6*d*.

Watts.—ESSAYS ON LANGUAGE AND LITERATURE. By THOMAS WATTS, of the British Museum. Reprinted, with Alterations and Additions, from the Transactions of the Philological Society, and elsewhere. In 1 vol. 8vo.

[*In preparation*

Wedgwood.—A DICTIONARY OF THE ENGLISH LANGUAGE. By HENSLEIGH WEDGWOOD, M.A. late Fellow of Christ's College, Cambridge. Vol. I. (A to D) 8vo., pp. xxiv. 508, cloth, 14*s*.; Vol. II. (E to P) 8vo. pp. 578, cloth, 14*s*.; Vol. III., Part I. (Q to Sy), 8vo. pp. 366, 10*s*. 6*d*.; Vol. III. Part II. (T to W) 8vo. pp. 200, 5*s*. 6*d*. completing the Work. Price of the complete work, £2 4*s*.

"Dictionaries are a class of books not usually esteemed light reading; but no intelligent man were to be pitied who should find himself shut up on a rainy day in a lonely house in the dreariest part of Salisbury Plain, with no other means of recreation than that which Mr. Wedgwood's Dictionary of Etymology could afford him. He would read it through from cover to cover at a sitting, and only regret that he had not the second volume to begin upon forthwith. It is a very able book, of great research, full of delightful surprises, a repertory of the fairy tales of linguistic science."—*Spectator*.

Wedgwood.—ON THE ORIGIN OF LANGUAGE. By HENSLEIGH WEDGWOOD, late Fellow of Christ's College, Cambridge. Fcap. 8vo. pp. 172, cloth. 3*s*. 6*d*.

Wheeler.—THE HISTORY OF INDIA FROM THE EARLIEST AGES. By J. TALBOYS WHEELER, Assistant Secretary to the Government of India in the Foreign Department, Secretary to the Indian Record Commission, author of "The Geography of Herodotus," etc. etc. Vol. I., The Vedic Period and the Maha Bharata. 8vo. cloth, pp. lxxv. and 576. 18*s*. Vol. II., The Ramayana and the Brahmanic Period. 8vo. cloth, pp. lxxxviii. and 680, with 2 Maps.

Whitney.—ATHARVA VEDA PRÂTIÇÂKHYA; or, Çâunakîyâ Caturâdhyâyikâ (The). Text, Translation, and Notes. By WILLIAM D. WHITNEY, Professor of Sanskrit in Yale College. 8vo. pp. 286, boards. 12*s*.

Whitney.—LANGUAGE AND THE STUDY OF LANGUAGE: Twelve Lectures on the Principles of Linguistic Science. By WILLIAM DWIGHT WHITNEY, Professor of Sanskrit, etc., in Yale College. Second Edition, augmented by an Analysis. Crown 8vo. cloth, pp. xii. and 504. 10*s*. 6*d*.

Williams.—First Lessons in the Maori Language, with a Short Vocabulary. By W. L. Williams, B.A. Square 8vo., pp. 80, cloth, London, 1862. 3*s.* 6*d.*

Williams.—Lexicon Cornu-Britannicum. A Dictionary of the Ancient Celtic Language of Cornwall, in which the words are elucidated by copious examples from the Cornish works now remaining, with translations in English. The synonyms are also given in the cognate dialects of Welsh, Armoric, Irish, Gaelic, and Manx, showing at one view the connexion between them. By the Rev. Robert Williams, M.A., Christ Church, Oxford, Parish Curate of Llangadwaladr and Rhydycroesan, Denbighshire. Sewed. 3 parts., pp. 400. £2 5*s.*

Williams.—A Dictionary, English and Sanscrit. By Monier Williams, M.A. Published under the Patronage of the Honourable East India Company. 4to. pp. xii. 862, cloth. London, 1855. £3 3*s.*

Wilson.—Works of the late Horace Hayman Wilson, M.A., F.R.S., Member of the Royal Asiatic Societies of Calcutta and Paris, and of the Oriental Society of Germany, etc., and Boden Professor of Sanskrit in the University of Oxford. Vols I. and II. Also, under this title, Essays and Lectures chiefly on the Religion of the Hindus, by the late H. H. Wilson, M.A., F.R.S., etc. Collected and edited by Dr. Reinhold Rost. 2 vols. cloth, pp. xiii. and 399, vi. and 416. 21*s.*

Wilson.—Works of the late Horace Hayman Wilson, M.A., F.R.S., Member of the Royal Asiatic Societies of Calcutta and Paris, and of the Oriental Society of Germany, etc., and Boden Professor of Sanskrit in the University of Oxford. Vols. III, IV. and V. Also, under the title of Essays Analytical, Critical, and Philological, on subjects connected with Sanskrit Literature. Collected and Edited by Dr. Reinhold Rost. 3 vols. 8vo. pp. 408, 406, and 390, cloth. Price 36*s.*

Wilson.—Works of the Late Horace Hayman Wilson. Vols. VI. VII. VIII, and IX. Also, under the title of the Vishṇu Puráná, a system of Hindu mythology and tradition. Translated from the original Sanskrit, anp Illustrated by Notes derived chiefly from other Puráṇás. By the late H. H. Wilson, Boden Professor of Sanskrit in the University of Oxford, etc., etc. Edited by Fitzedward Hall, M.A., D.C.L., Oxon. Vols. I. to IV. 8vo., pp. cxl. and 200; 344; 344; 346, cloth. 2*l.* 2*s.* [*Vols. V. and VI. in the press.*

Wilson.—Select Specimens of the Theatre of the Hindus. Translated from the Original Sanskrit. By Horace Hayman Wilson, M.A., F.R.S. Second Edition. 2 vols. 8vo., pp. lxx. and 384, 415, cloth. 15*s.*

CONTENTS.

Vol. I.—Preface—Treatise on the Dramatic System of the Hindus—Dramas translated from the Original Sanskrit—The Mrichchakati, or the Toy Cart—Vikrama and Urvasi, or the Hero and the Nymph—Uttara Ramá Cheritra, or continuation of the History of Ramá.

Vol. II.—Dramas translated from the Original Sanskrit—Maláti and Mádhava, or the Stolen Marriage—Mudrá Rakshasa, or the Signet of the Minister—Retnávali, or the Necklace—Appendix, containing short accounts of different Dramas.

Wilson.—The Present State of the Cultivation of Oriental Literature. A Lecture delivered at the Meeting of the Royal Asiatic Society. By the Director, Professor H. H. Wilson. 8vo., pp. 26, sewed. London, 1852. 6*d.*

Wise.—Commentary on the Hindu System of Medicine. By T. A. Wise, M.D., Bengal Medical Service. 8vo., pp. xx. and 432, cloth. 7*s.* 6*d.*

Wylie.—Notes on Chinese Literature; with introductory Remarks on the Progressive Advancement of the Art; and a list of translations from the Chinese, into various European Languages. By A. Wylie, Agent of the British and Foreign Bible Society in China. 4to. pp. 296, cloth. Price, 1*l.* 10*s.*

Yates.—A Bengálí Grammar. By the late Rev. W. Yates, D.D., Reprinted, with improvements, from his Introduction to the Bengáli Language. Edited by I. Wenger. Fcap. 8vo., pp. iv. and 150, bds. Calcutta, 1864. 3*s.* 6*d*

Slocum and Hancock Textbook on the Strength of Materials (Revised Edition)

By S. E. SLOCUM, Professor of Applied Mathematics in the University of Cincinnati, and E. L. HANCOCK, Professor of Applied Mechanics in Worcester Polytechnic Institute, Worcester, Mass. 8vo, cloth, xxxviii + 372 pages, $3.00.

SLOCUM AND HANCOCK'S "Textbook on the Strength of Materials" has been revised that it may be abreast of the most recent practical developments on the subject. The method of presentation has been simplified that the subject may be easily understood by average technical students of junior grade.

Considerable new material has been added. To facilitate numerical calculations a set of tables has been placed at the beginning of the volume. In Part I the most important additions are articles on the design of reënforced concrete beams, shrinkage and forced fits, the design of eccentrically loaded columns, the design and efficiency of riveted joints, the general theory of the torsion of springs, practical formulas for the collapse of tubes, and an extension of the method of least work to a wide variety of practical problems. This last includes a simple general formula for the shearing deflection of beams, never before published. Nearly one hundred and fifty original and practical problems have also been added to Part I.

In Part II the recent advances in the manufacture of steel have been given special attention, including the properties of vanadium steel, manganese steel, and high-speed steel. Reënforced concrete has also received a more adequate treatment, and the chapter on this subject has been thoroughly revised and modernized.

Smith The Teaching of Geometry *See Education, page 65*

Smith and Karpinski The Hindu-Arabic Numerals

By DAVID EUGENE SMITH, Professor of Mathematics in Teachers College, Columbia University, and LOUIS C. KARPINSKI, Instructor in Mathematics in the University of Michigan, Ann Arbor. 12mo, cloth, vi + 160 pages, illustrated, $1.25.

ALTHOUGH it has long been known that the numerals ordinarily employed in business, and commonly attributed to the Arabs, are